D1192878

BRAZIL

BRAZIL

TEXT BY SIMONA STOPPA

Contents

2-3 Christ the Redeemer overlooks Rio de Janeiro from the mountain of Corcovado, 2461 feet above sea level.

4-5 Lying between the sea and a tropical forest, Rio de Janeiro covers nearly 502 square miles.

6-7 Iguaçu Falls, in the state of Paraná, are among the most amazing water spectacles in all of Brazil.

8-9 Lençóis Maranhenses National Park consists of an immense stretch of lagoons and sand dunes sculpted by wind erosion.

11 Carnival in Rio de Janeiro offers an occasion to admire female samba dancers wearing sophisticated and colorful garb.

12-13 The impenetrable Amazon rainforest possesses the richest store of biodiversity in the world.

Introduction

Deus é Brasileiro, God is Brazilian. This is the belief of 201 million Brazilians, who are more than certain that only their land, so rich in beauty, joy and magic, could have been created by God in His own image. And indeed this country is an enormous treasure trove filled with dazzling marvels so astonishing as to be nearly hypnotizing.

The legendary Amazon rainforest, the boundless Pantanal wetlands in Mato Grosso do Sul and Mato Grasso, the fascinating cities of Brasilia and Fortaleza, and the country's seemingly endless shores are only some of the sights that have consistently stirred the imagination of travelers and explorers in Brazil. This is a land of magnificent white beaches, unspoiled rainforests, and metropolises that pulsate to the rhythm of captivating music.

Since Brazil occupies nearly half of South America, it is not surprising that it boasts five different habitats, tremendous biodiversity, and the greatest variety of ecosystems in the world. This abundance of nature allows locals and tourists alike to engage in diverse activities: horseback riding in the Pantanal wetlands, kayaking in the rivers of the Amazon rainforest, rock-climbing on craggy peaks that afford breathtaking panoramic views, whale-watching off the coast, surfing along beaches dotted with palm trees, and, finally, snorkeling among coral reefs or in the limpid waters of the country's many rivers.

The luxuriant nature of the countryside exists side by side with urban areas, be they small towns or megalopolises. A huge confederation of twenty-six states, Brazil is a giant that embraces chaos and peace, modern brilliance and a fascination with things ancient, the majesty of splendid structures and the dismal poverty of the *favelas*. One is left speechless by the beauty and grandiosity of utopian metropolises such as Brasilia, eclectic and overwhelming cities such as Rio de Janeiro, and ultramodern ones such as São Paulo. At the same time, one cannot but be deeply moved by cities such as Salvador de Bahia, which are rich in history, architecture, and tradition, or, like Manaus, blessed with elegant and fascinating colonial buildings that celebrate Art Deco and Art Nouveau, or, like Ouro

Preto, which are masterpieces of Baroque design. The common denominator of all these cities is the quest for height, as expressed by the great number of skyscrapers that stand out so elegantly against the sky.

Credit for Brazil's urban splendor is due above all to Oscar Niemeyer, the 20th-century architect who created many of the most futuristic buildings and complexes in cities such as Brasilia, São Paulo and Rio de Janeiro. Niemeyer's straight intersecting lines and plastic, sculpturesque forms stretching towards the sky have made him one of the great pioneers of Modernism. Indeed, his masterpieces can now be found all over the world.

The country's urban development certainly owes much to the country's economic growth. Since 2000, Brazil's gross domestic product has increased at an annual rate of 5%, allowing around 19 million Brazilians to attain middle-class status. Millions of new jobs have been created, and the unemployment rate has descended to a historic low. The impressive growth in many sectors of the economy demonstrates that Brazil is successfully achieving its potential of becoming the 'great nation of the future' as was already predicted in the mid-20th century. Much of the credit for its success should be given to President Lula, who in his two terms of office skillfully led the country to play a leading role on the international stage.

The vital energy of Brazilian cities is also found in the typical expressions of its culture: the acrobatic movements of the martial art, *capoeira*, and the frenetic rhythm of the samba; the *frevo* and *axé* music that animate Carnival; the percussion of *Candomblé* religious rituals; and the seductive melodies of the *bossa nova*, which combines the electric sound of Tropicalism and Música Popolar Brazileira, a form of urban pop that resounds with a rich repertory of influence.

Brazil is a variegated macrocosm filled with contrasts and surprises, the fruit of innumerable exchange and combinations, which, over the centuries have sown the fertile soil of this nation and allowed its myriad ethnic groups, cultures, and traditions to blossom in unison. The mixture of influence are like-

wise reflected in the local cuisine, which includes Portuguese olive oil, local manioc or cassava, Japanese sushi, okra (a vegetable of African origin), Italian pasta, German sausage, and Lebanese tabbouleh. Such amalgamations are reflected and described in the long tradition of literature and visual arts, from the satirical 17th-century poet Gregório de Matos Guerra to the 19th-century romantic poet Antônio Gonçalves Dias; from the principal 19th-century novels of Joaquim Maria Machado de Assis and the poetry of Carlos Drummond de Andrade to the 20th-century novels and short stories of Jorge Amado; from the oeuvre of the 18th-century architect-sculptor Antônio Francisco Lisboa to the photographs of Sebastião Salgado and the installations of the contemporary artist Ernesto Neto. The masterful works of these artists brilliantly convey the Brazilian spirit, vivacious and energetic but also permeated with *saudade* or melancholic longing, a nostalgic love for Brazil — a land in which one loses oneself, only to emerge richer in life and beauty.

16-17 A work in an exhibit at the São Paulo Biennial, which is second only to the Venice Biennial and features leading works of international contemporary art.

18-19 The historic center of Salvador de Bahia, known as Pelourinho, appears as a blaze of Baroque art, golden reflections, and pastel colors.

20-21 Surfers on one of the beaches in São Paulo at sunset.

TATUAGENS
CUSTOM
TATTOO
POINT
LA FAZENDA

Teatro
Restaurante
senac

sagittis egregie utitur · Hic psytaci uersicolores alieqz innumere a
ues fereqz monstruose · et Symiarum plura genera repperiuntur plu
rimaqz arbor nascitur que brasil nuncupata uestibus purpureo colo
re tingendis opportuna censetur ·
CIR CV
LV
S·O
CLI
CIRCV
CLIMA
TERRA BRASILIS
CLIMA
y. de santatã
y. de stã barbora
y. dos pargos
y. de madeyras

Brazil, a Bridge between Past and Future

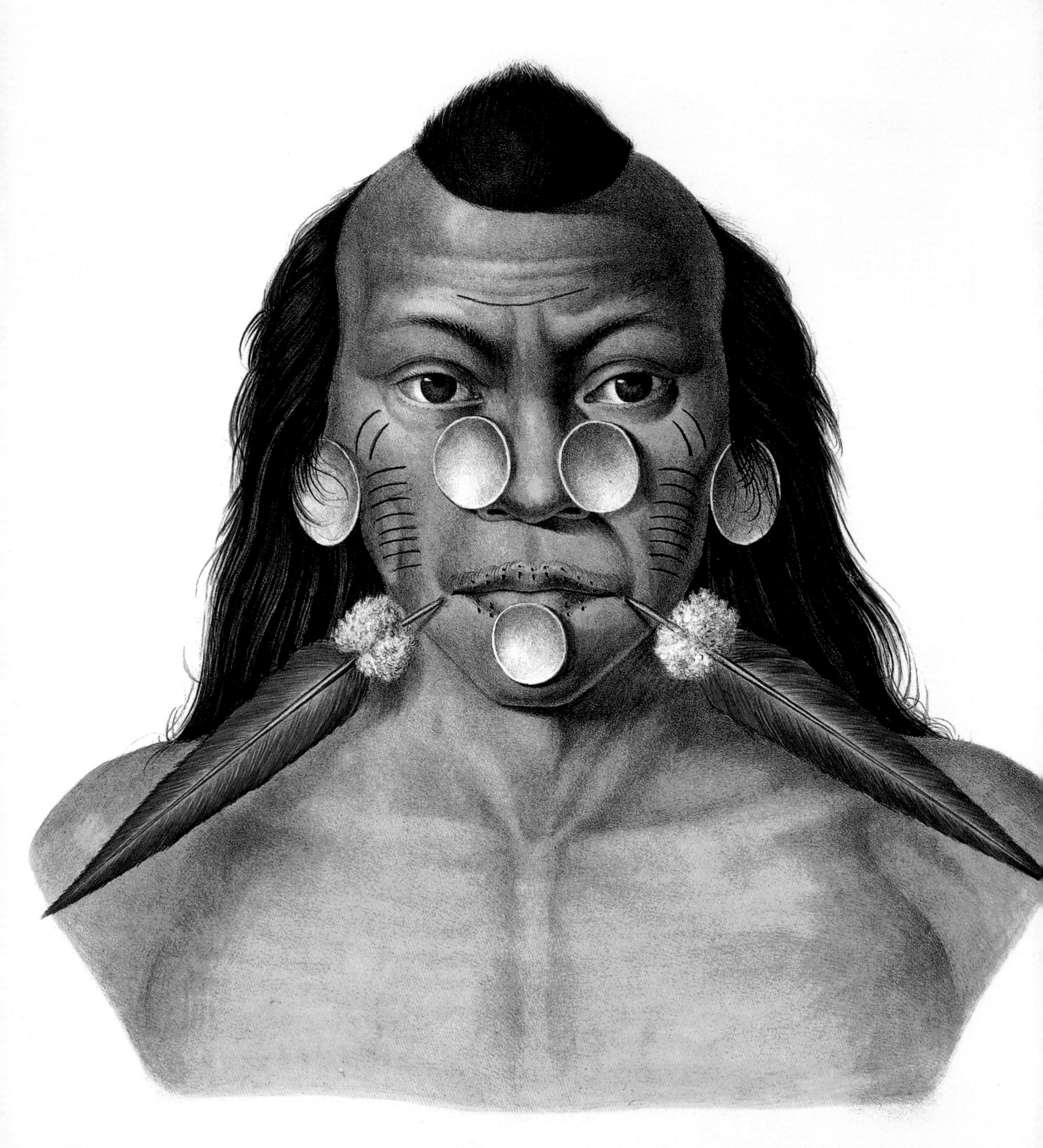

Philip. Schmid del.

THE PRE-COLUMBIAN INDIOS

Before the arrival of the Europeans, Brazil was inhabited by indigenous populations made up of various distinct ethnic groups that lived both on the coastline and in the interior, along large rivers. These semi-nomadic tribes, which subsisted on hunting, fishing and agriculture (mainly corn and manioc), did not leave behind written records or monuments, and the humid, torrid climate of the Amazon rainforest has destroyed nearly all trace of their culture, including their wooden implements. Consequently, what we do know about their existence in the period before the year 1500 is the result of deduction and reconstructions based on stone and bone tools used for hunting, fishing or war, pottery, and deposits of *terra preta*, or black earth, along the Amazon River. Recent excavations have brought to light the remains of large settlements with tens of thousands of dwellings, thus indicating the presence of a complex social and economic structure. Many of the 2000 or so tribes that existed back then were exterminated after the foundation of European settlements. Others underwent a drastic change in lifestyle after coming into contact with urban populations. Some, however, moved to isolated and remote Amazon regions, where they have preserved their cultural identity to this day. While only twenty years ago the Indios in Brazil numbered about one million, there are now only 300,000 of them, divided among 60 tribes.

22 A map of Brazil from Lopo Homem and Jorge Reinel's Miller Atlas (1519).

23 Dilma Vana Rousseff Linhares and Lula da Silva in 2010.

◁ *24 Portrait of an indigenous Brazilian, a member of the Maxuruna tribe.*

△ *25 The indigenous tribes of Brazil practice agriculture, fishing, and hunting, and lead a semi-nomadic life.*

EUROPEAN COLONIZATION

The 15th century marked the onset of Spanish and Portuguese overseas exploration. The discovery of the West Indies by Christopher Columbus triggered rivalry over the newly found territory between the two Catholic maritime powers. In 1494, in order to avoid war, Pope Alexander VI summoned Spanish and Portuguese ambassadors to Tordesillas, in Old Castille, and decreed the division of the New World into two empires. Thus, on 22 April 1500, the Portuguese explorer Pedro Álvares Cabral and his men set foot on Brazilian soil for the first time. In 1531, the king of Portugal, João III, sent the first colonists to Brazil. Many indigenous Indians were slaughtered by groups of adventurers (the so-called *bandeirantes*), wiped out by diseases brought from Europe, or died while working as slaves on sugar-cane plantations.

In 1534, the king divided the coastline into 14 *capitanias* or captaincies, which were entrusted to members of the gentry, who wielded total control over them and were required to pay tribute to their sovereign. Only two of these areas lived up to the king's expectations, however, so he decided to appoint Tomé de Sousa as the 'first governor of Brazil' and assign him the task of centralizing power and saving the *capitanias*. The new Governor General set up his headquarters in Salvador, which was the capital of Brazil until Rio de Janeiro assumed this role in 1763. As noted, many Indians died from European diseases, and so in order to make up for the lack of laborers on the plantations, the Portuguese decided to import slaves from Africa. The slave trade soon proved to be one of the most profitable enterprises in the colony.

26 On 22 April 1500, the explorer Pedro Álvares Cabral landed with his fleet at present-day Porto Seguro and took possession of Brazil for Portugal.

27 A map of Rio de Janeiro in a 16th-century painting.

Cot a Beure

Jardyns

Geneure

Jardyns

Lentree de la Riuiere de Geneure

Terre du Bresil

Lieues de chemin

la Grande ysle

Le grand bilage

escalle

Le Vray pourtraict de Geneure et du cap de frie

Le Cap

de frye

Tropic

a Lagadiço

SPANISH DOMINATION AND THE RETURN OF PORTUGAL

From 1580 to 1640, the period in which the Spanish and Portuguese crowns were unified, Brazil was administered by Madrid with the exception of a strip of the northeast coast (New Holland), which was under Dutch hegemony. In 1637, the charismatic Dutch Prince Johan Maurits of Nassau established the headquarters of his colony at Recife, from where he ruled as an enlightened ruler. In the meantime, the destruction of the Spanish fleet, the so-called Invincible Armada, by the English in 1588 as well as other major setbacks marked the beginning of Spain's irreversible decline. The Portuguese King João IV of Braganza took advantage of the situation and obtained sovereignty. He also regained control of the colony of Pernambuco after the Dutch were driven out of Brazil in 1654.

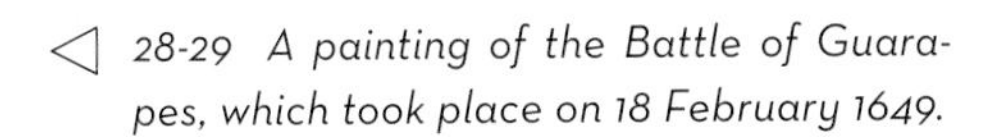

◁ *28-29 A painting of the Battle of Guarapes, which took place on 18 February 1649.*

▷ *29 An English fleet entering the bay of Rio de Janeiro.*

During this period, the country underwent major economic changes related for the most part to the discovery of large gold deposits in the states of Minas Gerais, Mato Grosso, Goiás, and in the zone south of the state of Bahia. The gold economy sparked a huge migration of Portuguese and native Brazilians from other regions, giving rise to the first noteworthy urban settlements and the foundation of historic cities in Minas Gerais, among these Ouro Preto (Black Gold). Furthermore, as betokened by the transfer of the nation's capital from Salvador to Rio de Janeiro (1763), the hub of Brazilian social-economic life shifted to the central-southern regions.

△ 30 *A diamond mine in an 18th-century watercolor.*

▷ 30-31 *This mid-17th-century painting depicts the home of a sugarcane plantation owner in northeastern Brazil.*

F. POST

THE FIRST STEPS TOWARD INDEPENDENCE

In the second half of the 18th century, the people of Brazil began to show signs of great dissatisfaction with colonial rule. The first independence movement was initiated by the patriot Tiradentes (Joaquim José da Silva Xavier, who was executed) and eleven other rebels. As things turned out, there was no need for a national liberation struggle against the mother country, since the Portuguese royalty—which had settled in Brazil after Napoleon's troops occupied Portugal in 1807—proclaimed the colony's independence in 1822. The protagonist of this decisive change was Dom Pedro, the son of King João VI of Portugal, who crowned himself emperor of Brazil as Pedro I.

△ 32 *In 1822, Portuguese King Dom Pedro proclaimed Brazil independent and appointed himself Emperor Pedro I.*

△ 32-33 *In 1818, João VI was proclaimed Titular Emperor of Brazil and Portugal in Rio de Janeiro.*

THE FIRST STEPS TOWARD THE REPUBLIC

On 7 April 1831, after years of severe instability marked by continuous popular uprisings, the population forced Pedro I to abdicate in favor of his son, Dom Pedro de Alcântara, who, being only five years old at the time, was flanked by a regency commission. This was a period of revolts placated through grants of autonomy to the individual provinces.

In 1840, Dom Pedro was declared an adult despite being only fifteen, and was appointed emperor as Pedro II the following year. This led to a long period of stability as he led the country for nearly half a century. Pedro II was a cultured ruler, who also proved to be an able politician. He paid particular attention to foreign policy, seeking the friendship of other countries, despite his failure—due to the legality of slavery in Brazil—to attain rapport with England. Indeed, because of this moral issue England went so far as to blockade Brazil's harbors in 1860. On the domestic front, Pedro II successfully embarked on a policy of economic expansion favorable to estate owners; rubber production and commerce grew, while large-scale coffee cultivation began after 1860.

Thanks to the huge number of African slaves who were imported to work on plantations, Brazilian society became markedly multiethnic, a development that has become its fundamental feature to this day.

It was only in 1888 that the government abolished slavery, an event soon followed by the collapse of the Brazilian Empire.

In 1889, a military coup d'état supported by the coffee plantation gentry overthrew the old empire, established the República Federativa do Brasil (made up of twenty autonomous states), and forced the emperor into exile.

35 *Pedro II ascended the throne in 1841 at the age of 16. The country enjoyed a long period of stability under his rule. A man of culture, he was also a skillful politician.* ▷

THE 'OLD REPUBLIC'

The first president of Brazil, the *paulista* Prudente de Morais, was elected directly by the people in 1894 with the support of the coffee producers. He coined the political phase *'do Café com Leite'* or 'coffee with milk,' referring to the power-sharing among politicians of the states of São Paulo (the largest coffee producer) and Minas Gerais (the leader in dairy production). The unrest caused by the small oligarchies of these two states led to the institution of the movement of the *tenentes*, members of the army, who, on 5 July 1922, organized their first act of rebellion on the beach of Copacabana. For the next eight years the coffee producers constituted the power elite, but after the disastrous Wall Street crash of 1929, the situation changed for good. The stock market collapse was followed by a significant drop in the coffee market; prices fell and many major Brazilian producers of the drink went bankrupt. All this marked the beginning of a decisive change in both the political and economic arena, and, in 1930, led to the takeover of power by the gaucho Getúlio Vargas, who, drawing inspiration from the Fascist regimes of Europe, governed the country by absolute rule. The contradiction between fighting in Europe on the side of the democratic nations in World War II (after an initial phase of neutrality, Brazil decided to collaborate with the Allies) while maintaining a dictatorial regime at home provoked the removal of Vargas by the military in 1954.

36-37 The populist dictator, Getulio Vargas, who assumed power in 1930, with army officers. ▷

THE DECADE OF DEMOCRACY AND THE MILITARY REGIME

In 1956, Juscelino Kubitschek was elected president and spent all his energy improving industrial production, which increased in Brazil by 80% in five years. However, his government also brought about terrible inflation, partly on account of the huge sums demanded by the construction of the new city of Brasilia on the Goiás plateau, which became the nation's capital on 21 April 1960.

Kubitschek was succeeded by the charismatic Jânio Quadros, an exponent of severity on the domestic front (he prohibited bikinis on beaches, for example), which led to strong criticism. Quadros was forced to resign after only seven months in office and was replaced by João Goulart of the Brazilian Labor Party, who promised social reforms and anti-corruption measures. Nevertheless, the high inflation rate inherited from the previous administrations did not allow his fragile democracy to survive. Another military coup occurred in 1964; this one was followed by no fewer than twenty-one years of dictatorship. During this era Brazil was ruled by presidents who were more or less severe, but all agreed on the need to combat Communism and corruption through repressive means. In 1969, the dictatorship reached its peak with a law that banned all politicians and judges of the opposition from holding public office and eliminated nearly all political parties, thus triggering armed clandestine resistance.

Paradoxically, this period of repression coincided with extraordinary cultural ferment; it was then that the musical phenomena known as *bossa nova* and Tropicalism, along with the New Cinema Novo of Roy

Guerra and Gláuber Rocha achieved world-wide success.

The years of dictatorship were also marked by a major economic boom; total acceptance of foreign capital and investment, loans granted by the International Monetary Fund, and the availability of huge numbers of underpaid laborers led to a period (1969-73) of economic growth, optimism and large-scale modernization, which were obviously vaunted by the regime's propaganda. The 1974 oil crisis, however, laid bare the fragility of the 'Brazilian miracle.'

As inflation soared, most of the population landed within that bracket of poverty to which 70% of it still belongs.

In 1974, Brazil elected a new president, the military leader Ernesto Geisel, who, well aware of the fact that it was impossible to govern through terror for any length of time, tempered repression with a policy of 're-democratization' that was continued by his successor, General João Baptista de Oliveira Figueiredo (1979-85).

◁ *38 President Juscelino Kubitschek participating in the proclamation of Brasilia as the new capital of Brazil (1960).*

△ *39 Students and other demonstrators march along the streets of Rio de Janeiro demanding an end to the government of Marshal Arthur da Costa e Silva.*

THE CONSOLIDATION OF DEMOCRACY

Reactionary backlashes and attempts by the military to adopt the strategy of terrorist attacks were in vain as they only helped consolidate the democratic movement, which by now was irreversible. In 1984, the movement organized the campaign known as *Diretas Já!* (Direct Elections Now!). The following year was marked by a great surprise; Tancredo Neves, the opponent of the military leaders, was elected president and millions of Brazilians gathered in squares to celebrate the end of the dictatorship. A shadow was cast over the return to democracy by the unexpected death of Neves, who was succeeded by Vice President José Sarney (1985-89). Sarney's mandate coincided with a period of uncontrollable inflation that contributed to Brazil's enormous foreign debt, which, in 1990, amounted to an appalling 115 billion dollars. However, Sarney passed a law that granted voting rights to the illiterate, who until then had been excluded from all political elections. The direct presidential elections of 1989—the first that can be regarded as truly democratic—saw the triumph of the 40-year-old Fernando Collor de Mello, who defeated the left-wing Luiz Inácio 'Lula' da Silva by a slim margin. After two years of ruinous economic programs, rampant nepotism, and unprecedented corruption, Collor was obliged to resign after being impeached with a parliamentary vote of 441 'ayes' to only 38 'nays.' In 1992 he was replaced *ad interim* by Vice President Itamar Franco, who governed the country honestly and competently. His best achievements lay in the economic sector, where he initiated a process of stabilization by introducing a new currency, the *real*. In 1995, Franco was succeeded by the sociologist and professor Fernando Henrique Cardoso, who was supported by a wide range of political forces, including the historic right wing. With the new *Plan Real*, a project for monetary consolidation aimed at blocking ungovernable inflation, albeit temporarily, Cardoso corrected the balance of trade. Yet, between 1989 and 1996, two million jobs were lost and the serious problems of agrarian reform continued unresolved. Despite the situation, Cardoso won a second term in 1998, but another economic crisis in 1999 led to the *real*'s devaluation. In 2001, due to the country's slow economic growth and an energy crisis, the International Monetary Fund had to step in with an extraordinary loan of 30 billion dollars so that Brazil would not be gravely affected by the disastrous economic crisis in neighboring Argentina.

41 In 1995, the sociologist and professor Fernando Henrique Cardoso, supported by a wide range of backers and representative social groups, succeeded Itamar Franco as president. ▷

On 27 October 2002, 'Lula,' the leader of the Workers' Party, won the second ballot of the elections and became an extremely popular left-wing president. He took office on 2 January 2003, stating that his primary objectives were to revive economic growth and curb domestic and foreign debt so that the country could play a leading role in the revival of the South American Common Market (Mercosur). Once he had gained the trust of the International Monetary Fund and local entrepreneurs, Lula tried to combat social inequality, hunger, organized crime, and narcotics trafficking through agrarian reform and structural changes in the tax and pension systems. Among other things, he enacted the *Bolsa Familia* program, which provided relief for 11 million families. This move allegedly reduced the poverty rate in Brazil by 27%. In 2005, Brazil paid off its 15-billion-dollar debt to the International Monetary Fund well before the deadline, thus raising its status to one of the leading nations in terms of economic growth. Lula was reelected president for a second four-year term in 2006, which ended in 2010. During this time, the economic expansion of Brazil continued, and the left-wing leader's popularity enjoyed an all-time high.

In 2010, the president bequeathed an economically healthy country to the new president, Dilma Vana Rousseff Linharesa, politician and economist. However, even Linhares' Brazil felt the effects of the world crisis; while in 2010, the country's Gross Domestic Product had increased by 7.5%, in 2011 the rate dropped to 2.7%, and in 2012 to only 0.9%. All the same, Brazil replaced the United Kingdom as the world's sixth largest economy in 2012 and is now preparing to host two of the world's leading sports events: the 2014 World Soccer Cup and the 2016 Summer Olympic Games.

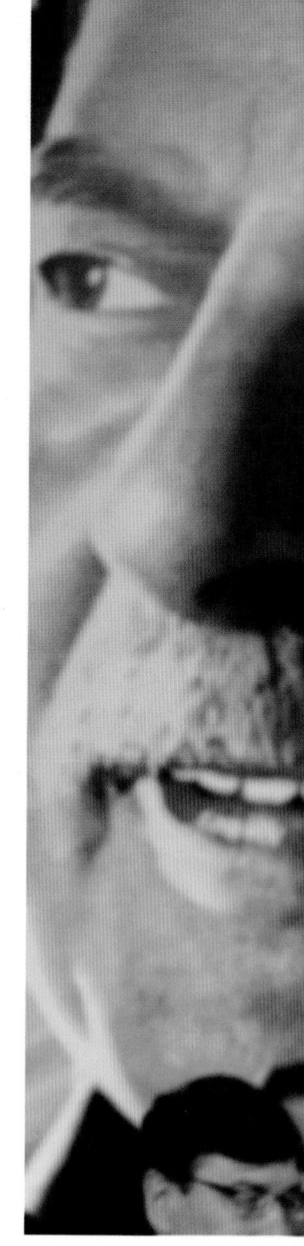

42-43 Elected in a second ballot in 2010, Dilma Vana Rousseff Linhares became the first female president of Brazil. ▷

The Triumph of Nature

Unparalleled biodiversity of both flora and fauna as well as an astounding variety of landscapes and ecosystems—this is the 'portrait' of Brazil's physical environment, which includes the largest rainforest in the world, immeasurable wetlands and semideserts, and miles and miles of extraordinarily beautiful beaches.

With a total surface area of 3,281,868 square miles (almost half of South America), Brazil has five different terrestrial ecosystems: Amazonia, Mata Atlântica, Caatinga (semiarid land), Cerrado (the central savanna) and the swampy zones of Pantanal. The Amazon rainforest occupies approximately half of the country and contains 20% of the world's plant, over 10% of its mammal, and 15% of its birds species. It is thus a veritable sanctuary of biodiversity for our planet, and is nurtured by the majestic Amazon River. The Mata Atlântica, or Atlantic rainforest, is older than Amazonia and developed independently. Unfortunately, unsustainable exploitation of natural resources and agricultural as well as urban expansion have led to the near destruction of this area. Indeed, its present-day surface area of 13,513 square miles amounts to a mere 7.4% of the original 193,051 square miles. In order to preserve the flora and fauna of the Mata Atlântica, UNESCO has created numerous reserves that also protect the indigenous Indios communities that live in the area. While the Caatinga and Cerrado are 'open' and nearly arid regions—albeit rich in life—the same cannot be said for Pantanal, the largest wetland in the world. A vast marshy plain lying at the very center of South America and extending from Brazil to Bolivia and Paraguay, Pantanal was formed by an inland marine depression. One of the most uncontaminated and unexplored regions in Brazil and the final refuge for certain animal species that are well on their way to extinction, Pantanal is almost totally submerged beneath water for half the year and is thus a sort of natural outdoor laboratory for millions of species that use it as a meeting ground. A true floating paradise, the territory hosts a labyrinth of rivers, lakes, lagoons, and marshes that conceal incredible, marvelous plants and animals, including jaguars, deer, caimans, and anacondas.

44 Spectacular Iguaçu Falls are the most overwhelming expression of nature's force in Brazil.

45 The jaguar, with its sinuous, elegant movements and precious spotted coat, is the undisputed king of the Amazon rainforest.

47 A large group of butterflies, swept by the wind, rests on a sandy and rocky coast washed by the waves.

AMAZONIA: THE 'LUNGS' OF OUR PLANET

The Amazon River (3902 miles long) is unrivalled with regard to the number of its tributaries, no fewer than 1100, and the size of its basin, the drainage area of which covers one-third of all of South America. Although not as long as the longest river in the world, the Nile (4132 miles), the Amazon has an average discharge greater than that of any other river—around 7,062,933 cubic feet per second. Formed by the confluence of the Marañón and Ucayali Rivers in Iquitos, Peru, the Amazon begins its course parallel to the Equator and flows into the Atlantic Ocean.

Its drainage basin corresponds to Amazonia (2,702,715 square miles, 65% of which lie in Brazil), which extends over nine countries and is the world's richest ecosystem and home to 60,000 plant species, 1,300 bird species, and over 400 species each of mammals, amphibians, and reptiles. The entire Amazon River Basin has roughly 5000 species of trees alone, 50,000 of flowers, and around 30 million of insects. Among the most interesting Amazonian creatures are jaguars, tapirs, spider monkeys, armadillos, caimans, alligators, river dolphins, boa constrictors, anacondas, toucans, and scarlet macaws.

Brazil also boasts the Mata Atlântica (Atlantic rainforest), which now covers only 7% of its original surface area, and which too is home of many endemic species. Of the 26 species of primates that live here, 21 are endemic, as are 900 of the more than 2000 species of butterflies and most of the 600 species of bird. The 20,000 plant species in this ecosystem (half of which are endemic) constitute 8% of the world's flora.

Recent research conducted by FUNAI (Fundação Nacional do Índio or National Foundation for Indian Affairs), has estimated that 67 tribes of Indios living in Brazilian Amazonia have no contact whatsoever with the external world. These are the so-called isolated populations. One of the largest and most primitive are the Yanomami. The Terra Indígena Yanomami, in the northern part of the state of Amazonas, covers 37,317 square miles and is the largest of the tribe's reserves. There its members, still using stone utensils, pottery, animal hides, and plants, lead a semi-nomadic existence, quite removed from what we consider modern reality.

49 The Amazon River is a huge freshwater highway that has flowed through Peru, Colombia, and Brazil for thousands of years. ▷

50 The appearance of the river changes during the rainy season, when its waters overflow the banks, creating bends, islands, and lagoons.

50-51 Amazonia is an endless stretch of water and forest vegetation with a population of one person per 0.386 square mile.

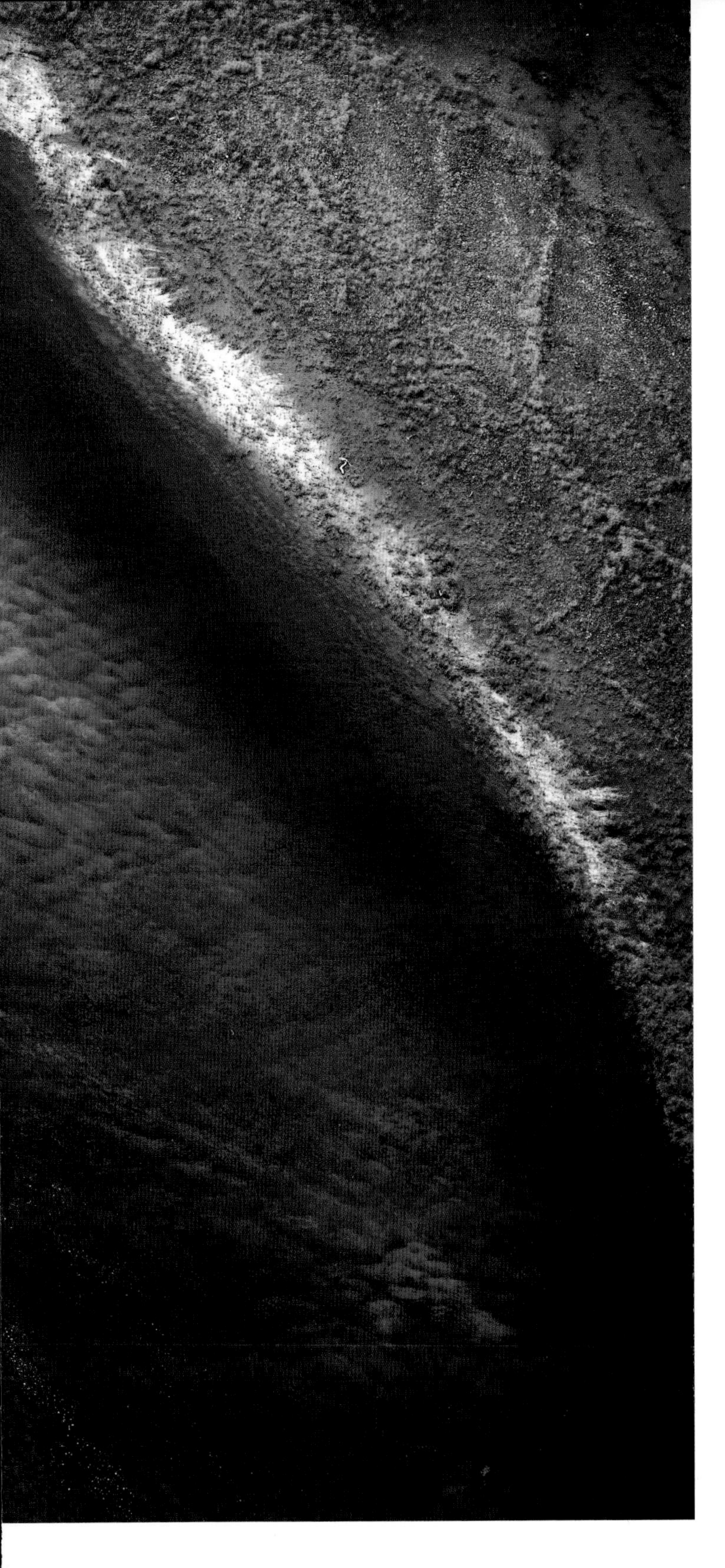

◁ 52-53 *The Amazon River is a paradise for explorers and researchers from all over the world as well as a major communication route for local populations.*

◁ 54-55 *The integrity of Amazonia is constantly threatened by deforestation.*

▽ 55 *Home to tens of thousands of animal and plant species, the Amazon rainforest is the richest ecosytem in the world.*

56-57 *The vast Amazon rainforest in the morning mist.*

58 The Amazon rainforest is so thick that little sunlight can penetrate it. Hence its magical atmosphere. ▽

58-59 One of the animals most characteristic of Amazonia is the boa constrictor, whose long, sinuous body blends seamlessly with tree branches. ▷

60 An evergreen plant native to tropical regions, Heliconia is one of the 60,000 species of flora identified to date in the Amazon rainforest. △

61 One of most curious inhabitants of Amazonia is the Cacajao calvus *or bald uakari, a small bald-headed monkey with a red face.* ▷

◁ 62 *The plumage of the* Ara macao *or scarlet macaw is green, red, yellow, and blue.*

△ 63 *The scarlet macaw is about 35 inches long; its pointed tail takes up more than half its length.*

64 The Amazon milk frog, so named because of its color, is the rarest of the innumerable amphibians in Amazonia. △

64-65 The Corallus caninus *or emerald tree boa hangs from branches for hours waiting for its prey.* ▷

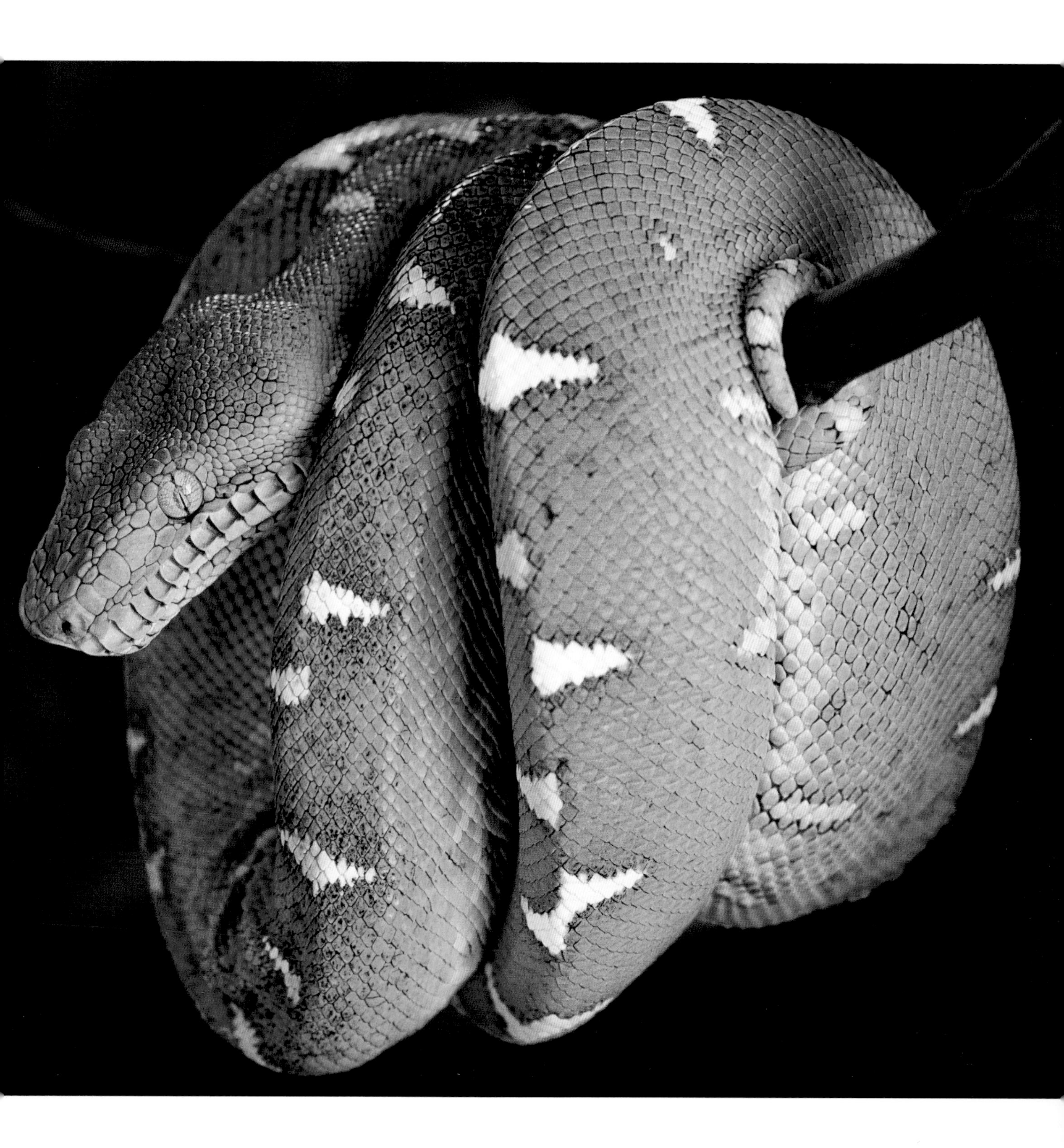

PANTANAL AND IGUAÇU: MIRACLES OF WATER

About 600 million years go, during the Quaternary Period of the Cenozoic Era, a powerful shift in the Earth's crust led to the creation of the Andes mountain range as well as the formation of a deep (1968-2296 feet) depression within the continent that the indigenous populations call Mar de Xaraés. Present-day Pantanal, which lies in Bolivia, Paraguay, and Brazil, is all that remains of this internal sea, which, after drying up, became first a lake. then an alluvial plain of approximately 81,081 square miles. Rainfall flows from the plateaus to this ecological paradise, forming the Paraguai River (with a depth of up to 194 feet and an average discharge of 5,050 cubic feet of water per second) and its tributaries. During the rainy season (November-March) the rivers here overflow, flooding most of the lower region of Pantanal and creating *cordilheiras* or small islands, where numerous animals gather. The rivers are also populated by about 300 species of fish and no fewer than 658 species of birds, including the tall (as much as five feet) jabiru stork with its scarlet collar and black head and beak. Mammals and reptiles dispute dominion over the territory. While the former include capybaras, the Pantanal marsh deer, and the elegant jaguar, the latter are much more plentiful, amounting to nearly 10 million species, including small and large caimans as well as fine specimens of anaconda.

Discovered in 1542 by the Spanish adventurer Don Álvar Núñez, Iguaçu Falls are yet another marvelous 'water spectacle.' Shared by Argentina and Brazil, the waterfalls are formed by the Paraná and Iguaçu Rivers and were created about 120 million years ago by a fracture in the Earth's crust. They comprise 275 'stages,' down which flow about 523,972 cubic feet of water per second. The average height of the falls is 213 feet, the maximum is 295 feet, and the spray displays a perpetual rainbow. In 1939, Iguaçu Falls was enclosed in the middle of Iguaçu National Park, a 656 square miles forest, which, besides providing an opportunity to admire the fabulous waterfalls, offers a network of simply breathtaking nature trails. Some of these have views over the Itaipú Dam (in the Paraná River), one of the largest in the world, which provides electricity to all of Paraguay and central-southern Brazil.

67 Pantanal, a vast wetland in Mato Grosso—a magical world of variegated light—populated by birds, mammals, and a great number of fish species. ▷

68 The fruit of the waterlily grows beneath the surface; after blooming it breaks away from the plant's core and spreads seeds. △

68-69 The lagoons of Pantanal are carpeted with enormous waterlilies that decorate a seemingly endless body of water. ▷

70-71 The pluvial environment is the favorite habitat of the Amazon river dolphin, a freshwater cetacean that acquires a particular pink hue when reaching adulthood. ▷

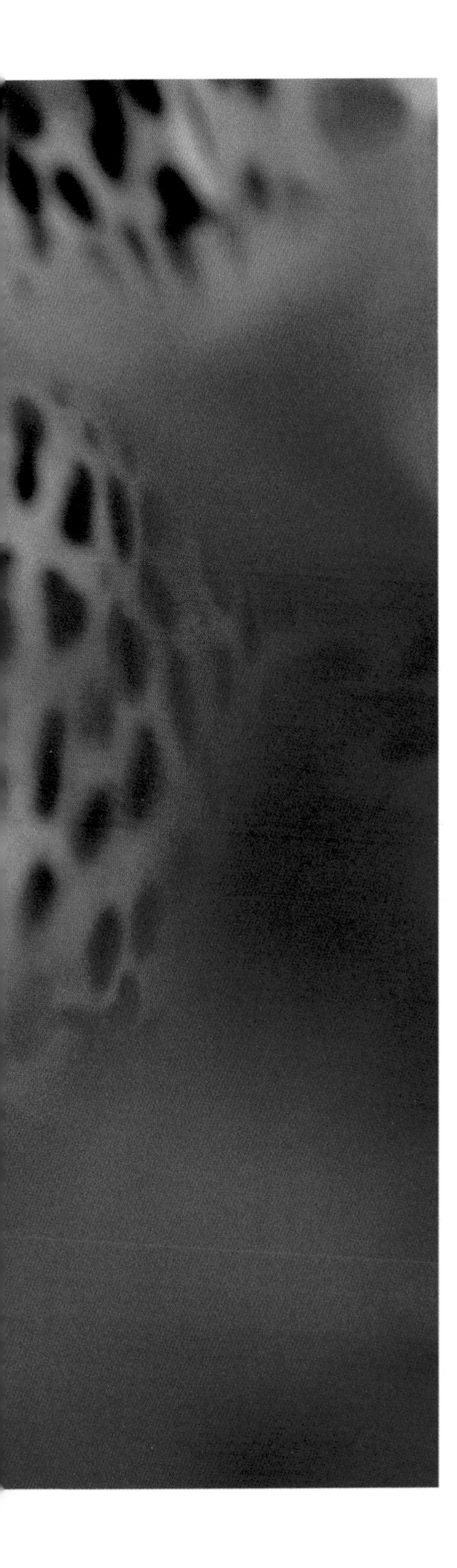

◁ 72-73 *Jaguars are the largest felines in South America and direct rivals of such large creatures as the anaconda and caiman.*

△ 73 *By suffocating it with its coils, a boa constrictors is able to swallow prey that is larger than its head.*

74 Lagoons and vegetation-covered marshes make Pantanal an ideal habitat for the caiman. △

74-75 At 154 pounds, the capybara is the largest rodent in the world. ▷

△ 76 top The marsh deer is the largest deer species in South America and is quite easy to spot in Pantanal.

△ 76 bottom Giant anteaters are among endangered Latin American species; one of their last refuges is the area of Pantanal.

▷ 77 The waters of Pantanal offer a virtually unlimited reserve of food to the 700 species of birds that live in the area.

◁ *78-79 Toucans flying through the humid air rising from the lagoons in the early morning, the ideal moment for hunting small freshwater fish.*

▽ *79 Wood ibises darken the sky as they take off and–an instant later–dive into the water to catch their prey.*

80-81 The huge Iguaçu Falls, situated on the Brazil-Argentine border, are the largest phenomenon of this kind in Latin America. ▷

WILD, HIGH-ALTITUDE LANDS

The epitome of biodiversity 'par excellence,' Brazil boasts a variety of absolutely unique habitats; it is a land of white beaches, vibrant metropolises, and uncontaminated rain forests, not to mention majestic mountains and endless plateaus.

Without a doubt, the Brazilian state that best displays this diversity is Mato Grosso, one of the most important and fragile ecosystems on our planet. The region closest to Bolivia and Paraguay, the Mato Grosso was once considered Brazil's Wild West, where one would encounter Indios, poachers, gold prospectors, and naturalists. Nowadays, this area, divided into two states, Mato Grosso and Mato Grosso do Sul, still preserves its wild features and harbors the most fascinating plant and animal species in the country: jaguars, caimans, anacondas, giant otters, and capybaras, as well as macaws, toucans and jabirus. After Pantanal—a wide alluvial plain ideal for observing and studying wild animal species—the Chapada dos Guimarães National Park is the main attraction in Mato Grosso. The park lies on a rocky plateau around 3281 feet above sea level and offers what are certainly the best panoramic views in all of Brazil. The two highlights of the park are the amazing Veu de Noiva (Bridal Veil) Falls, 282 feet high, and Cidade de Pedra ('Stone City'), a series of jagged sandstone formations that resemble stone temples.

While on the one hand, the Mato Grosso is a treasure chest of beauty, on the other, it is part of an even greater source of beauty, the Cerrado. This natural environment lies on the central highlands of Brazil and includes other states besides Mato Grosso, such as Goiás and the southern part of Maranhão. Typical areas in the Cerrado are covered with savannas, open pasture strewn with trees or covered with brush, palm groves or thick forest. This habitat is the home of 800 bird species and a wide gamut of flora— over 10,000 species, 45% of which are endemic. The state of Goiás, which takes an active part in preserving this incredible ecosystem, is the least visited region in Brazil for reasons wholly unjustified. In fact, it boasts the spectacular Chapada dos Veadeiros National Park, which covers 251 square miles and is absolutely enchanting with its tall waterfalls, steep canyons, natural waterholes, as well as hills and groves of *Butia capitata*, jelly palm trees, which are scattered like oases throughout the area. Other sights are the Vale da Lua (Valley of the Moon), the São Mi-

83 With their breathtaking views, the plateaus of Mato Grosso remind one of the Far West in the United States. ▷

guel River, and extraordinary rock formations with numerous craters created by erosion.

The same magical atmosphere reigns in the state of Minas Gerais, a sort of plateau with a view of the ocean and abounding in parks near the states of Rio de Janeiro and São Paulo. Serra do Cipó National Park is one of the most beautiful and uncontaminated of these, with vegetation typical of the Cerrado and a terrain consisting of tall mountains and high-altitude pasture. At lower altitudes, waterfalls and river valleys covered with fern and orchids are populated by wolves, monkeys, anteaters, jaguars, and bats.

The southern portion of Minas Gerais is equally fascinating; hidden among the green hills that rise along the southern border are spas with therapeutic waters, small valleys, and a village, São Thomé das Letras, situated on a hill, which is deemed sacred due to mysterious inscriptions found in nearby caves. Off the beaten track, are a nature reserve and the biological station of Caratinga, famous for having prevented the extinction of the southern muriqui, a very rare woolly spider monkey with exceptional social habits based on strong mutual support and fraternal interaction. This species resembles humans quite closely and, in fact, possesses many values that could more properly be considered human.

◁ 84-85 *Cidade de Pedra or Stone City in Mato Grosso rises majestically over the surrounding forests.*

◁ 86-87 *Tableland, known as* chapada *in Brazil, alternates with ragged massifs dotted with thick vegetation.*

△ 87 *Bridal Veil Falls, 282 feet high, are the main attraction in Chapada dos Guimarães National Park.*

◁ *88-89 The tall mountains of the state of Roraima are located at the triple border of Brazil, Venezuela, and Guyana.*

▽ *89 Standing atop the Brazilian plateaus with their nearly surreal views, one seems able to touch the sky and climb over the clouds.*

UNSPOILED COASTS AND BEACHES

Four-thousand-six-hundred-and-three miles—this is the total length of the Brazilian coast, in which large cities, small towns, sprawling beaches, nature parks, islands, and different ecosystems alternate.

Traveling along an ideal route starting from the north, the first stretch of coastline one encounters is that of the immense Nordeste or northeast region. At the first stop, one may see the states of Piauí and Maranhão come together in a spectacular site created by the delta of the large Parnaíba River: a surface area covering about 1042 square miles and abounding in land and marine landscapes, spectacular sand dunes, and rich mangrove thickets.

Heading south, one enters Maranhão and eventually comes to the charming National Park of Lençóis Maranhenses with its ever-shifting dunes and small emerald-green lagoons. From it extend another sixty-two miles of ragged and uninhabited coastline, which has been declared a nature reserve and includes a very rich marine park, Parcel de Manuel Luís.

The most spectacular marine paradise in Brazil, however, is the Fernando de Noronha archipelago, 224 miles from Natal and designated a national marine reserve in 1988. The archipelago is simply spellbinding; its volcanic cliffs hang over golden beaches, while the intense emerald sea is home to schools of spinner dolphins with long rostra that 'perform' pirouettes and other acrobatic maneuvers.

Returning to the land and heading southward, one finds another charming natural jewel: Pipa Beach in Natal, the capital of the state of Rio Grande do Norte. Here enchanting stretches of sand, parts of which lie in sheltered coves, are flanked by green palm groves, white sand dunes, and tall cliffs—a true ecological sanctuary, in which schools of dolphins can engage in typical play and sea turtles can swim in peace.

There is certainly no end to the beautiful scenery along the 559 miles of coastline in the state of Bahia, especially along the stretch between Todos os Santos Bay and the capital city, Salvador de Bahia. Here, shorelines bordered by palm trees—such as those at Barra, Pituba, Piatã and Itapoan—welcome tourists

91 The Lençois Maranhenses are an astounding, boundless stretch of sand dunes and transparent lagoons in the state of Maranhão. ▷

with cafés, music, and sailboats typical of the region. Todos os Santos Bay is the largest in Brazil: 386 square miles with 56 islands, lush vegetation, and architectural ruins that bear witness to the area's rich past. The largest of these islands, Ilha de Itaparica, is covered with vast swaths of Atlantic tropical forests, mango trees, and coconut palms; to the west lie mangrove forests (an ecosystem known as Pantanal Baiano), and protecting the island on the east are impressive coral reefs. Further south is the breathtaking sight of the famous Morro de São Paulo (St. Paul Hill), surrounded by wonderful sand, palm trees, and crystal clear water. A few miles south, one comes to Abrolhos Marine National Park, an archipelago of five islets of volcanic origin, with rocks shaped by wind erosion, fine sand, emerald-green water, and coral reefs that shelter the beaches from ocean currents. This is the 'stage' on which appear large humpback whales, migratory mammals capable of traveling up to 15,534 miles in one year in order to reproduce in warm waters.

The first sight in the state of Rio de Janeiro is the Costa do Sol, an area with sand dunes, lagoons, and white beaches, on which chic Búzios—known as the Saint-Tropez of Brazil—attracts hordes of people with its trendy vibe. At a good distance from the coast and its fashionable atmosphere, lies the Ilha Grande. Once a refuge for pirates, then for lepers, and finally a prison for dangerous criminals, the large island with its splendid tropical beaches has remained unspoiled and is now completely reserved for pedestrians.

Past the Costa Verde and the colonial-style town of Paraty, one arrives in the state of Santa Caterina with its 348 miles of sunny coastline, marvelous sea beds, an ideal surf, and deserted beaches. The half-moon shaped Praia do Rosa (Pink Beach) is absolutely magical, surrounded as it is by lagoons and hills covered with wild vegetation. The beauty of the site is world-famous; UNESCO, in fact, places it in the 'Club of the Most Beautiful Bays in the World.' Like the entire Brazilian coast, it is a magnificent place that never fails to bewitch visitors.

93 *Fernando de Noronha is an archipelago in the Atlantic Ocean with beautiful beaches situated about 217 miles from the Brazilian coastline.*

94-95 *Known as the Grand Canyon of Brazil, the Morro Branco is the most famous beach of Beberibe, 55.7 miles south of Fortaleza.*

96-97 White sand and crystal clear water are the chief highlights of the more than 4603 miles of Brazilian coastline. ▷

◁ 98-99 *The Brazilian coast is lined with sand that can be as high as 131 feet for hundreds of miles.*

▽ 99 *The zone known as Praia da Pipa attracts many tourists, who love to dart among the dunes in small 4-by-4 cars.*

◁ 100-101 *Endless sand dunes dominate the beach of Punta Grossa in the state of Ceara.*

◁ 102-103 *The coast, like the interior, is a habitat abounding in various animal species, such as the brown booby, which lives on the archipelago of Fernando de Noronha.*

△ 103 *The beaches of the islands of Fernando de Noronha are an ideal spot for surfers who love tall, majestic waves.*

104-105 Although the spinner dolphin usually lives in the open sea, it sometimes approach the coasts of Brazil, where it 'performs' amazing acrobatic 'acts.'

106-107 The beach of Dos Hermanos in the archipelago of Fernando de Noronha ablaze at sunset.

The Contrasts of Urbanization

Brazilian cities can be either modern, even utopian, or old and colonial, rich in contrasts but always original and irresistible. The country's urban architecture, much of which is colonial (16th-18th century), reflects the most salient moments of Brazilian history with brightly colored Renaissance and Baroque buildings and houses often decorated with high-quality stuccowork. From the early 19th to the early 20th century, Brazilian architecture was influenced primarily by the French. Interest in and enthusiasm for Neo-Classicism led to the construction of grandiose and monumental works such as the Amazonas Theater in Manaus and the Theatro da Paz in Belém. Art Nouveau became popular in the late 19th and turn of the 20th century, giving rise to such splendid constructions as the interior of the tearoom and pastry shop in Rio de Janeiro's Confeitaria Colombo. The 1930s witnessed the rise of Art Deco and the concomitant emergence of a new generation of Brazilian architects headed by the charismatic Oscar Niemeyer and influenced by the Modernist ideas of Le Corbusier. Among the most striking examples of this style are the impressive statue of Christ the Redeemer and the country's principal railway station, both in Rio de Janeiro, and the majestic buildings along President Vargas Avenue in Belém.

This gamut of styles is characterized by different but absolutely compatible approaches to urban planning. Examples range from the 'surreal' architectural project of Brasilia to the perfect mixture of skyscrapers and nature in Rio de Janeiro, from the ultramodern megalopolis of São Paulo to the highly refined colonial setting of Salvador de Bahia. Yet this is not all. In addition to these vast metropolises—one of whose distinctive features is the unsettling coexistence of impressive buildings and squalid *favelas*—are small jewels of an authentic Brazilian cast, towns like Manaus, Ouro Preto, Paraty, among so many others.

With its Baroque churches, chapels and monasteries, and brightly colored houses that burst with energy, Olinda, for example, is a veritable open-air colonial museum. Situated on a *morro* (hill) 4.3 miles from Recife, it is one of the best-preserved colonial towns in Brazil and was placed on the UNESCO World Heritage List in 1982. Founded in 1535, it was the first capital of the state of Pernambuco and is now a picturesque, romantic, and lively city thanks to its creative population, artist ateliers, and street musicians, as well as its red tile roofs and striking bell towers.

Nearby Recife, on the other hand, is a variegated example of European influences. Now the capital of Pernambuco in northeastern Brazil, the town was named after the Portuguese word *recifes* or 'coral reefs,' a direct reference to the reef that encircles it like a crown. Also known as the 'Brazilian Venice' due to the forty bridges that span its rivers, Recife is marked by strong contrasts between old and new, and has harbored Portuguese, Spanish, Dutch, and French populations, which have left their mark over the years by constructing bridges, fortresses, Neo-classical palaces, buildings, and museums.

Porto Alegre (also known as Porto do Sol or Port of the Sun, and Cidade Sorriso or Happy City) is a rich, sophisticated harbor city lying along the shores of the Lagoa dos Patos (Lake of the Ducks), an immense freshwater lagoon. With over seventy neighborhoods, it boasts a richly varied architectural heritage; its Baroque, Neo-classical and Modernist buildings make it a fine example of Brazil's architectural eclecticism.

Another unique city is São Luís, the only one in Brazil founded by the French. The capital of the northeastern state of Maranhão and the focal point of the colonial style of the Nordeste region, this city was built on the eponymous island and is separated from the mainland by narrow canals. São Luís truly resembles an outdoor exhibition; its historic center contains a host of colonial-style buildings with paved patios, pastel façades faced with *azulejos* (typical glazed tiles), finely carved doors, and wrought-iron balconies. Here too there are ruins of French architecture, a church with Byzantine features, and numerous narrow cobblestone streets lined with art galleries and handicraft workshops.

FUTURISTIC BRASILIA

Modern and utopian Brasilia is the result of exceptional town planning promoted in the 1950s by President Juscelino Kubitschek, who moved the capital here from Rio de Janeiro.

The geographic position of the city had already been strategically studied in 1922. Founded on Planalto Central, a plateau 3845 feet above sea level, it was to promote the development of the central region of Brazil by integrating all its various states. Through his creation of a Federal District in the state Goiás, at the very heart of the country, Kubitschek made an old Brazilian dream come true.

Brasilia was laid out in 1956-60. The chief urban planner of the city was Lúcio Costa, who drew inspiration from the theories of the father of modern architecture, Le Corbusier. Most of the public buildings were designed by Oscar Niemeyer, while Roberto Burle Marx was commissioned to work on the landscaping. The result of this cyclopean operation was Brasilia's

108 The Rio de Janeiro skyline is dominated by the Sugar Loaf, a mountain 1300 feet high with a peculiar conical shape.

109 A view of Pelourinho, the historic quarter of Salvador de Bahia, a UNESCO World Heritage site.

112-113 The buildings of the Senate and Chamber of Deputies in Brasilia consist of two domes, one convex, the other concave, separated by two parallelepiped structures.

designation as a UNESCO World Heritage Site in 1987, the only city built in the 20th-century to receive this honor. The project called for detailed planning of residential and commercial zones, industrial areas, a financial center, an area for hotels and others for hospitals. Lúcio Costa claimed that the project resulted from "the primary gesture of someone who marked out a site in order to take possession of it: two axes intersecting at right angles, the very sign of the cross." The cross had to be adapted to the topography of the site and to the planned artificial lake of Paranoá, created to offset the low humidity that occurs in certain periods of the year. The city therefore assumed the shape of an airplane, though some people prefer to interpret it as an eagle on the wing.

The Monumental Axis (Eixo Monumental), the main artery of the metropolis, is lined with the city's principal sights, including the Square of the Three Powers (Praça Dos Três Poderes) with its three monumental buildings designed by Oscar Niemeyer (1957-59), which are dedicated to the 'three powers' of the state: executive (Palácio do Planalto, the presidential palace), judicial (Supreme Federal Court), and legislative (National Congress). The last of these buildings has two semi-spherical domes, the larger one of which is convex and houses the Chamber of Deputies, and the smaller one, concave, which serves as the seat of the Senate. A pool and two vertical buildings twenty-eight-stories (328 feet) tall, which house the administrative activities of the two legislative bodies, round off this impressive architectural complex. The Square of the Three Powers is enhanced by sculptures made by Bruno Giorgi and Alfredo Ceschiatti, while the rest of the city is beautified by the works of artists such as Athos Bulcão, Marianne Peretti, Victor Brecheret, and Roberto Burle Marx, all of which blend in perfectly with the city's architecture.

The visionary genius of Niemeyer can be seen in other monuments and buildings in Brasilia, such as the futuristic Metropolitan Cathedral (1958-60), a circular edifice supported by 16 curved columns from which hang splendid stained-glass works by Marianne Peretti; the Ministries Esplanade, which includes the Ministry of Foreign Affairs (1962) and the Ministry of Defense (1977); the Memorial to Juscelino Kubitschek (1980), the National Theater (1958), the Alvorada

Palace (the President's residence, 1958), the National Museum and Library (2006), and the Memorial to the Native Populations (1982). Another impressive work along Eixo Monumental is the 754-foot television tower that affords spectacular views of the city and Lake Paranoá, which today is also used as a recreation and sports area.

The 'airplane wings' of the city, each of which is 4.3 miles long, are known as the North and South Wings. Each contains residential areas, schools, churches, and separate commercial streets. The city's division into well-defined sectors, with broad avenues and tall trees, is quite visible. With time, however, the city's Pilot Plan revealed its limitations, particularly in terms of the mistaken estimate of a population of 200,000 inhabitants. While in 1960 the population was ca. 140,000, by 2010 it was well over 2.5 million. Furthermore, though the city was planned when automobiles were already quite common, the original plan did not call for traffic lights; overpasses or tunnels were built to avoid crossroads. To alleviate the problems caused by this peculiar feature, a large number of pedestrian crossings were added to the avenues and, more recently, two subway lines were established.

What makes Brasilia even more fascinating are five parks, which include the Botanical Garden, the large Parque da Cidade (City Park) and the Parque Nacional de Brasília, a nature reserve covering 115 square miles also known as Água Mineral (Mineral Water) because of its many pools and springs. Brasilia also has a large Zoological Garden featuring 253 endangered representing all of South America.

An entirely Italian curiosity is the sanctuary dedicated to Don Giovanni Bosco, with 52-feet high pointed arches supporting huge stained-glass windows of various hues of blue. Don Bosco occupies a special place in the hearts of the citizens of Brasilia because already in 1833 he had a prophetic dream of a futuristic city in its present location: "....When they will excavate the mines hidden in these hills, the Promised Land will appear, flowing with milk and honey. It will be of inconceivable prosperity....". And so it happened. The Brazilians had the daring, courage and strength to realize a promised city that arose from nothing, as President Kubitschek never failed to assert.

◁ 116 *The sculpture of Os Guerreiros, situated in the Plaza of the Three Powers, is a tribute to the workmen who built the capital city.*

△ 117 *The entrance to the headquarters of the Armed Forces Command in the Federal District of Brasilia.*

118 Alfredo Ceschiatti's statue, Blind Justice, *which stands before the building of the Supreme Federal Court, is one of the many artistic and architectural works scattered throughout the city.* △

119 A portrait of Juscelino Kubitschek–president of Brazil from 1956 to 1961 and 'founder' of Brasilia–before the federal courthouse. ▷

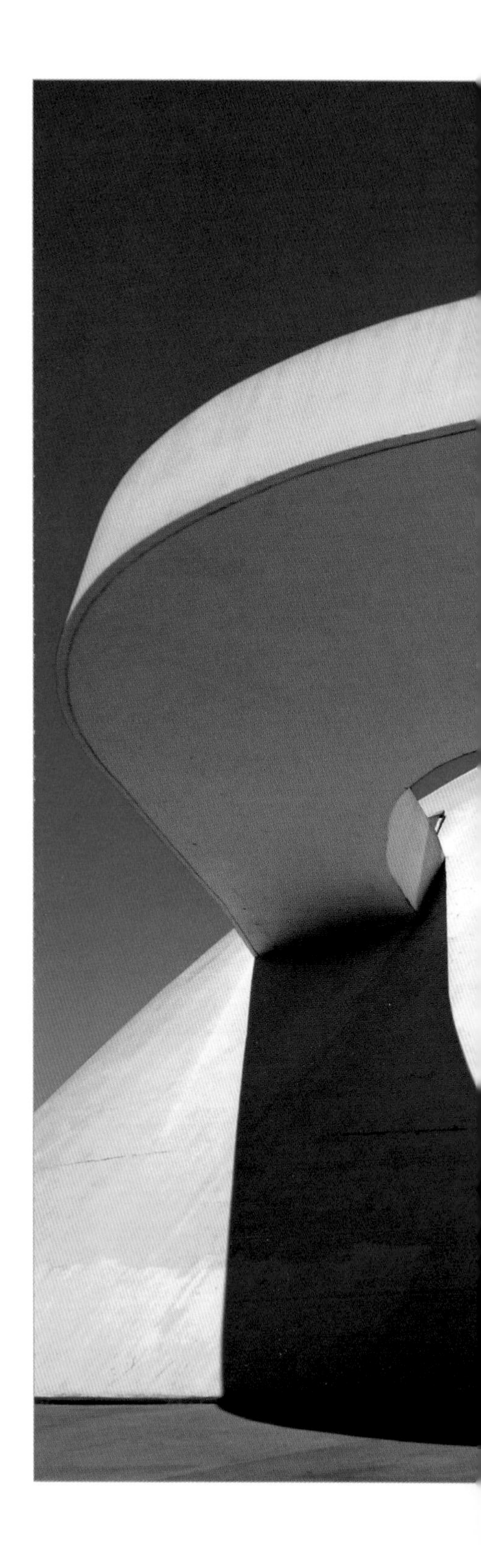

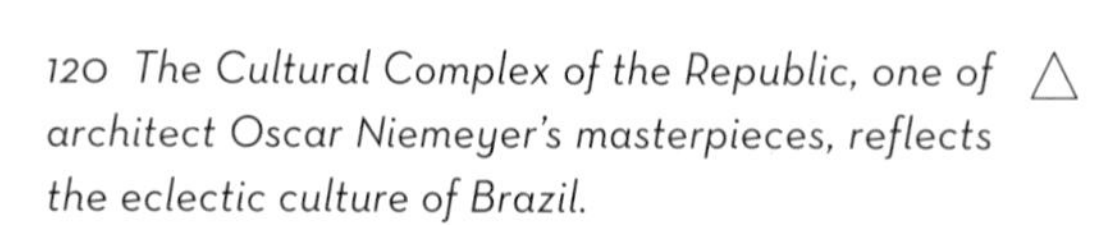

120 The Cultural Complex of the Republic, one of architect Oscar Niemeyer's masterpieces, reflects the eclectic culture of Brazil. △

120-121 In addition to the National Library, the Cultural Complex boasts the ultramodern National Museum of the Republic, which houses precious art collections. ▷

122-123 Another example of Oscar Niemeyer's genius is the futuristic Cathedral of Brasilia, constructed of reinforced concrete and glass. ▷

△ 124 top L'Eixo Monumental is the principal artery of the city, running past all of its main attractions.

△ 124 bottom The stadium in Brasilia is also an architectural marvel. Named after Mané Garrincha, a legend of Brazilian soccer, it has a seating capacity of over 70,000.

▷ 125 Brasilia is flanked by the Preto River on the east and the Descoberto River on the west.

SENSUAL RIO DE JANEIRO

Captivating, sensual, paradoxical: Rio de Janeiro, the '*Cidade Maravilhosa*' or Marvelous City, which many people consider the most beautiful in the world.

When the Portuguese arrived at charming Guanabara Bay, just north of the Tropic of Capricorn, on 1 January 1502, they mistook it for the mouth of a river and thus called it '*Rio de Janeiro*,' that is, 'January River.' Facing the Atlantic Ocean, the city unfolds—among skyscrapers and *favelas*—along plains stretching between rugged granite mountains and hills covered with tropical forests, the so-called *morros*. The mountains offer various lookouts with exceptionally beautiful panoramic views. The best of these is from the summit of Corcovado, which is 2461 feet high and hosts the symbol of Rio: the 125-foot statue of Christ the Redeemer with outstretched arms, a sight that literally leaves one breathless. Built in the 1920s to a design by the French sculptor Paul Landowski, the monument was declared one of the New Seven Wonders of the World in 2007. It never fails to astound the viewer.

Majestic and impressive, the mountain of Corcovado lies in Tijuca Forest National Park, the world's largest urban forest as well as a UNESCO World Heritage and International Biosphere site. From it the view is simply spectacular; rocky peaks with perpendicular sides rise along the coast, commanding attention and awe. The most famous of these is Sugarloaf Mountain (Pão de Açúcar), 1299 feet high, the fascinating conical shape of which dominates the city skyline. It offers a magnificent view of the southern and central parts of the city. On the one side, lie the beaches of Copacabana, Ipanema and Leblon; on the other, the bay of Botafogo, Flamengo, the historic center of Rio, the city of Niterói, and the Rio-Niterói Bridge, which overlooks Guanabara Bay. At sunset, the Sugarloaf becomes utterly romantic when night begins to fall and the multicolored lights of the promenade reflected in the sea make for a truly magical sight.

One must descend to 'ground level' and leave behind this phantasmagorical series of views from on high in order to grasp the multitudinous facets of the city with its population topping 6 million, and its metropolitan area accommodating 12. Rio harbors a life of strong and vivid contrasts: extreme forms of both wealth and poverty; upscale neighborhoods side by side with over 600 squalid *favelas*; white, brown and black citizens; lush nature and cold, lifeless urban sprawl; peaceful well-being and violence; exuberance and *saudade*, or melancholy.

127 With his outstretched arms, Christ the Redeemer symbolically embraces Rio de Janeiro, the former capital of Brazil (1763 to 1960). ▷

Divided into 160 quarters, Rio de Janeiro encompasses four districts: the Center, North, South, and West. A walk in Centro is tantamount to a journey through past and present. Here modern skyscrapers tower over elegant colonial buildings, museums, Baroque churches, and lively pedestrian squares. An outdoor architectural museum, Rio's historic area is a dazzling treasure trove: the National Library, built in the Neoclassical style with Art Nouveau elements in 1910; the National Fine Arts Museum; the huge Confeitaria Colombo, a famous pastry shop with Belle Epoque furnishings; the Theatro Municipal, modeled after the Paris Opéra; and the Cathedral of São Sebastião (St. Sebastian), whose imposing pyramidal structure contains four huge stained-glass panels. This is the *carioca* megalopolis. But there is also the Mosteiro de São Bento, a richly decorated monastery dedicated to St. Benedict and a masterpiece of Baroque architecture; the Neoclassical Church of Igreja da Candelária (Our Lady of Candelária) with frescoes and marble decoration; the splendid November XV Square and colonial Santa Teresa quarter, distinguished by its old houses, alleyways, and small squares.

The South District of Rio is the richest and most famous. Its long, winding white and golden beaches, Copacabana, Ipanema, as well as Leblon, Catete, Flamengo, and Botafogo, are the dream of millions of visitors and help enhance the city's mythical aura.

The West District is the largest in the city, a site of huge urban expansion. In a state of continuous growth, it has rich and poor neighborhoods, as well as *favelas* and state housing developments, including the infamous Cidade de Deus or City of God.

Yet it is the vast and thickly populated North District that is considered the soul of Rio de Janeiro. This is the home of all major samba schools, the Sambódromo (a sort of parade ground for this dance) and the mythical Maracanã stadium, one of the largest in the world, with a seating capacity of nearly 100,000. Although it does contain middle- and upper-class quarters, the district is historically the poorest in the city, with a significant number of *favelas* on the hills of Tijuca.

Another major feature of Rio de Janeiro is its status as queen of entertainment and recreation from New Year's Day to Carnival. This is when locals laugh to the beat of the samba, a sensual dance strongly influenced by African rhythm, that is not only entertaining but stirring because as the spiritual cornerstone of Brazilian culture, it commands belief.

129 Constructed in the early 20th century, the Municipal Theater in the Cinelandia quarter displays an eclectic mixture of architectural styles inspired by the Paris Opéra. ▷

MUSICA
MCMVI MCMIX
C.GOMES
G.VERDI
THEATRO MUNICIPA

◁ 130-131 *On the peak of the Corcovado, the 125-foot statue of Christ the Redeemer rises dramatically over the city below.*

△ 131 *Christ the Redeemer keeps watch over the glorious Maracanã, the world's largest soccer stadium with a seating capacity of nearly 100,000.*

132 The megalopolis of Rio de Janeiro consists of 160 barrios (neighborhoods) and covers a total surface area of 468 square miles. △

132-133 The urban sprawl extends both horizontally and vertically—the reason for the creation of an aerial tramway that runs as far as Sugar Loaf mountain. ▷

134-135 Copacabana is a 3.7-mile-long beach framed by the sea on one side and a host of skyscrapers on the other.

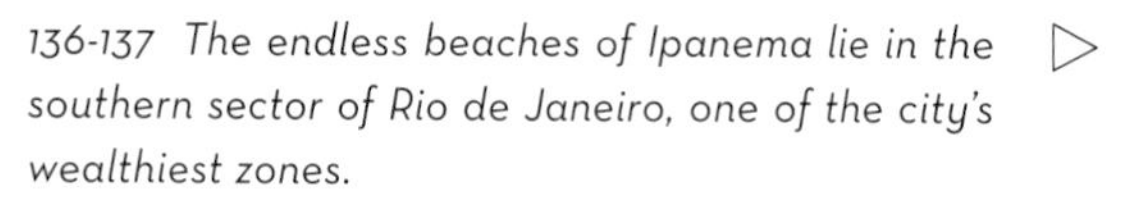

136-137 The endless beaches of Ipanema lie in the southern sector of Rio de Janeiro, one of the city's wealthiest zones.

138-139 The renowned architect Oscar Niemeyer conceived the futuristic Contemporary Art Museum in Rio de Janeiro as a flower blossoming from a vase, represented by the pool of water below. ▷

140 The green, yellow, and blue Brazilian flag waving along the seaside on a carpet of golden sand. △

140-141 The long promenade behind the Copacabana was laid out with the traditional 'Portuguese pavement.' ▷

MASSAGE

◁ 142-143 *Other famous beaches besides Copacabana are Ipanema, Arpoador, Tijuca, and Praia do Pepe—unique spots where one can get a whiff of the typically zesty atmosphere of Rio.*

▽ 143 *These spectacular sand castles are only one of the many present-day artistic expressions covering the beaches of Rio de Janeiro.*

144 Art depicts the city. In this painting, a tram running from the upper part of Rio passes through the gigantic urban areas known as favelas.

145 The Escadaria Selaròn—created by the Chilean artist Jorge Selaròn as a tribute to the Brazilian people—is a stairway decorated with over 2000 colored tiles.

◁ 146-147 *In Rio de Janeiro art steps out of museums and galleries to beautify the walls of the city with elegant and sophisticated murals.*

△ 147 *The yellow Santa Teresa Tram (known as Bonde) connects the downtown area with the Santa Teresa district via the old Carioca Aqueduct, which was converted into a bridge for the tram.*

148 The ceiling of the ultra-modern Cathedral of São Sebastião is decorated with thousands of tiny tesserae of colored glass that shimmer in the light. △

149 A reflection of the 348-foot Metropolitan Cathedral of Rio in the glass walls of a downtown skyscraper. ▷

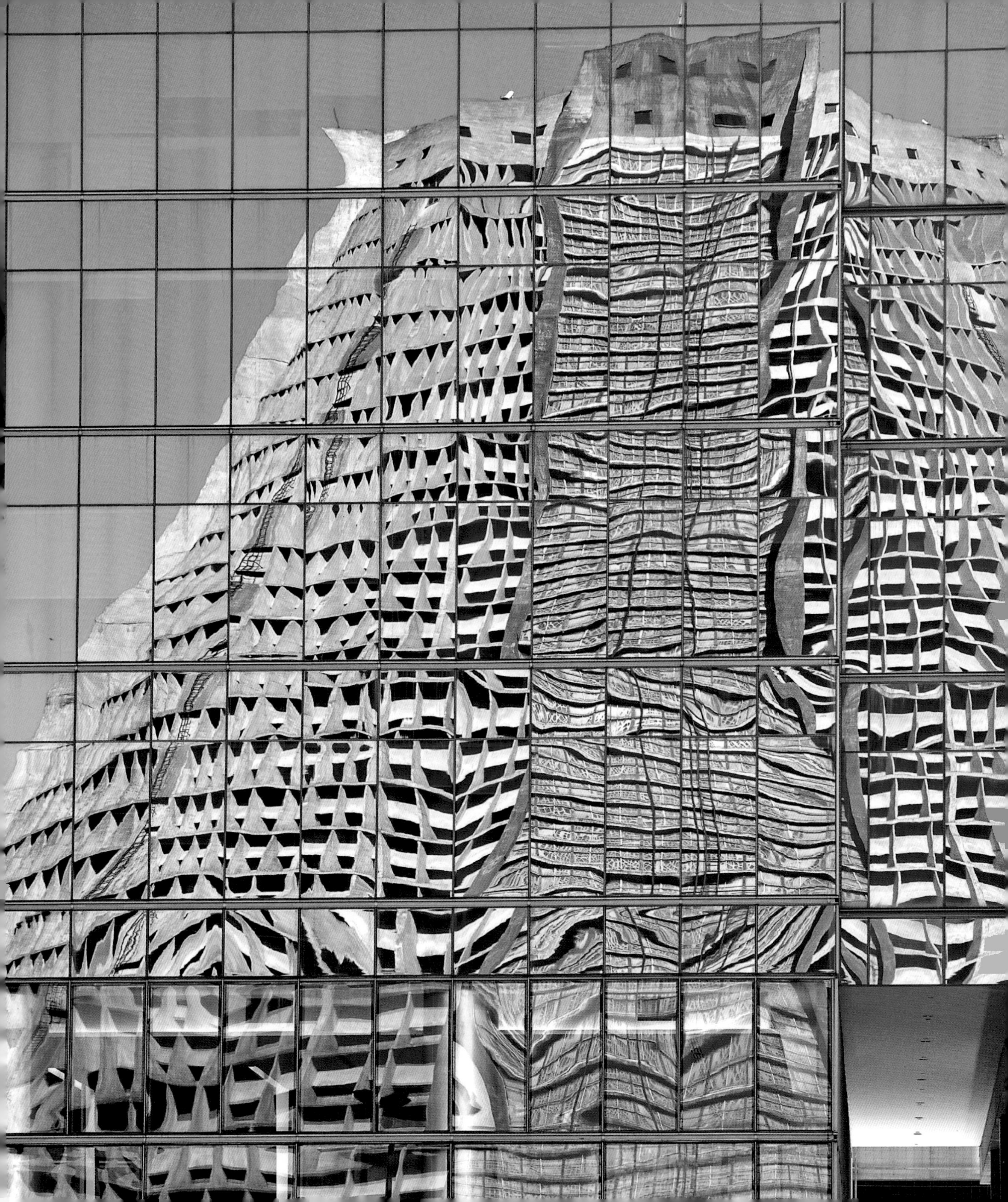

◁ 150-151 *The gigantic Metropolitan Cathedral, already ablaze with color in the early evening, blends in perfectly with the city's animated light life.*

152 Colonial buildings, Baroque churches, and charming alleys provide an incredible mixture of styles in the historic center. ▽

152-153 According to tradition, the cornerstone declaring the foundation of Rio del Janeiro in 1565 was laid on Sugar Loaf Mountain. ▷

154 Excellent cuisine and cheerful company are the main features of many restaurants in Rio. △

155 The Confeitaria Colombo, a historic tearoom and pastry shop in the heart of town, has been an important part of the city's cultural and artistic heritage for over a century. ▷

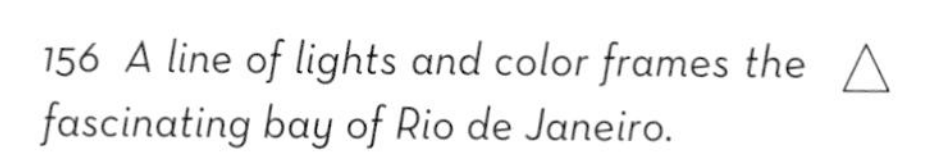

156 A line of lights and color frames the fascinating bay of Rio de Janeiro. △

156-157 The large beach known as Copacabana, illuminated both day and night, attracts thousands of visitors. ▷

DYNAMIC SÃO PAULO

Seemingly endless, densely populated, pulsating with life, São Paulo is the largest megalopolis in the Southern Hemisphere; its metropolitan area has a population of over 20 million. Situated a few miles south of the Tropic of Capricorn, it extends along the plateau of the Serra do Mar mountain range, approximately 2625 feet above sea level.

The origins of the city date to 1554, when Jesuit missionaries founded the village of São Paulo de Piratininga, where they also built a college and church. The actual urban nucleus was formed in 1711. A century later, in 1822, after the proclamation of Brazil's independence, the city became the capital of the state of São Paulo.

By the late 19th century, thanks to the cultivation and exportation of coffee, the city wielded a great deal of economic power. For this reason, after slavery was abolished in 1888, hordes of Italian and Spanish immigrants arrived in Brazil seeking work on plantations. They, in turn, were followed by the Japanese, who at present number 1.5 million persons—the largest Japanese community outside their country.

In the early 20th century, a sudden drop in coffee prices led local entrepreneurs to invest in industrial development and the establishment of new factories, thus attracting additional waves of immigrants. The city is still considered the Brazilian melting pot par excellence, as its population is 70% white, 24% colored, 4% African-American, and 2% Asian.

The population explosion triggered drastic inequality and differences between the city's outlying quarters, with their concentration of dozens of *favelas* and working-class areas housing millions of persons, and the more central ones with their fashionable streets, fine restaurants, and luxury homes. In recent years demographic expansion has gradually slowed down, but São Paulo has nonetheless retained its indisputable superiority over other large cities in Brazil thanks to its finance, industry, and culture. It is, in fact, the home of the Stock Exchange, large multinational firms, important bank organizations, consulates, business tourist agencies, and 75% of the country's trade fairs and congresses. In terms of culture, the city boasts a venerable and distinguished university tradition (including the Universidade de São Paulo with its renowned Faculty of Law);

159 *At São Paulo, the* Hand *sculpture of the Latin America Memorial complex designed by Oscar Niemeyer celebrates the culture and spirit of the countries of Latin America.* ▷

concerts given by international artists; leading fashion and design shows as well as sports events (including São Paulo Fashion Week and the Formula 1 Grand Prix); and numerous theaters, movie theaters, and museums.

A stroll along the streets of this city is a unique experience: traffic, smog, a striking multitude of people, stalls, street art, and modern buildings soaring next to historic structures, are some of the many features experienced on a daily basis. São Paulo grew at breathtaking speed with no plan. Rather than following a grid, its streets merge in a tangle of networks that radiate from the historic center in concentric circles. Almost all the tourist attractions are concentrated between the oldest area and Avenida Paulista, the principal artery, which is lined with modern skyscrapers. To the north of this avenue is the 'Centro.' This consists of Republic Square (and its surroundings, including the Copan Building, designed by the renowned Oscar Niemeyer); the zone known as Bela Vista, inhabited primarily by Italians; the restored cultural area of Luz; the Japanese quarter of Liberdade; and the old historic heart of the city around Praça da Sé. The last of these is overlooked by the enormous Neo-Byzantine Metropolitan Cathedral, an capable of accommodating up to 8000 persons. In the surrounding area is São Francisco de Assis, one of the best preserved colonial churches in the city; the Belle-Epoque-style Mercado Municipal or Municipal Market with its stained glass and large domes; and the Triângulo zone, which is dominated to the north by the impressive Mosteiro de São Bento, one of the oldest monasteries in São Paulo.

South of the Avenida Paulista lie the quarter of the Jardim Paulista, filled with greenery, sophisticated restaurants, and luxury boutiques; the Jardim Europa residential zone; the elegant ramparts of the neighborhoods Vila Olimpia and Itaim Bibi; and the vast Parque do Ibirapuera, the largest in the city. Nearby is the São Paulo Art Museum (1968), one of the chief cultural centers in the country, renowned for its architecture and the largest collection of Western art in all of Latin America. Near the park, fine art lovers can visit the Modern Art Museum, Contemporary Art Museum, State Painting Gallery and the Biennial– a patrimony at the disposal not only of tourists, but also of the local middle class, which is the largest and most cultured in Brazil.

161 The Octávio Frias de Oliveira Bridge in São Paulo is braced by cables and has two curved tracks supported by a single mast.

162-163 The grandiose city is reflected in the pools of Ibirapuera Park, which is around 0.77 square miles.

164-165 *The ultra-modern and densely urban center of São Paulo.* ▷

◁ 166 *The Pinheiros River is one of the navigable waterways passing through the entire megalopolis of São Paulo.*

△ 167 *Conceived by the designer Roberto Burle Marx and dotted with works by Oscar Niemeyer, Ibirapuera Park was inaugurated in 1954.*

168 Santos Beach boasts a beachfront garden over 3 miles long, which, according to the Guinness Book of World Records, is the longest in the world.

168-169 The Morumbi quarter next to the Pinheiros River is the most elegant and sophisticated zone in São Paulo.

Hilton

170 Victor Brecheret's Monument to the Bandeirantes is situated in Ibirapuera Park and represents a row of chained slaves pulled by two horses. △

170-171 The monument celebrates the memory of the Indios, who were hunted and reduced to slavery in the 16th century by the Paulistas. ▷

◁ 172-173 *Ibirapuera Auditorium, designed by Oscar Niemeyer, is trapezoidal. Its entrance resembles a long red tongue rippling in the wind.*

△ 173 *The circular Parliament of Latin America designed by Oscar Niemeyer bears witness to the strong bonds among the people and states of South America.*

◁ *174 Sculptures by the artist Antony Gormaley on display at the Banco do Brazil Cultural Center, one of the most popular museums in the world.*

△ *175 The Estado de São Paulo Art Gallery is the oldest artistic institution in the city. Built in 1905, it houses vast 19th-century art collections.*

176-177 Art pervades every corner of São Paulo; even the main post office hosts photograph and art exhibitions.

METROPOLITAIN

◁ 178-179 *Even the shops and boutiques in São Paulo are designed by leading architects and designers. Here we see the showroom of the Firma Casa firm, the façade of which is covered with plants in aluminum vases.*

△ 179 *Large volumes and minimal furnishings are virtually obligatory in contemporary Brazilian design, which pays special attention to the interior.*

180-181 Due to its creative approach, this shoe shop in downtown São Paulo attracts customers during São Paulo Fashion Week. ▷

◁ *182-183 São Paulo nightlife exudes a unique atmosphere with scintillating lights that accentuate the city's urban structures.*

▽ *183 Ramos de Azevedo Square viewed from above with the Municipal Theater at its center.*

MANAUS, THE PARIS OF THE TROPICS

Along the banks of the Negro River, near its confluence with the Amazon, lies Manaus, the capital of the state of Amazonas, a transport hub for the region's river network, the capital of ecotourism, and gateway to the Amazon rainforest.

Manaus, whose name derives from the indigenous Manáo (Mother of the Gods) tribe, enjoyed its golden age when the American Charles Goodyear (who invented the vulcanization process for natural rubber) and the Irishman John Dunlop (who patented rubber tires) learned that huge quantities of Brazilian rubber trees could be found in the area. Consequently, this town of merely 5000 inhabitants was inundated by thousands of immigrants seeking work as *seringueiros* or rubber gatherers, a phenomenon that transformed Manaus into a large city with all its usual striking contrasts.

Today, side by side with impressive skyscrapers lies a seemingly endless sprawl of shantytowns with wooden dwellings. Yet Manaus is also called the 'Paris of the Tropics' due to its European-style buildings. The Amazonas Theater, for example, was modeled after the Garnier Opéra in Paris and was begun in 1884 in what could be termed an eclectic Neo-Renaissance style. With its pink façade, a dome clad with 36,000 colored ceramic tiles, roof tiles imported from Alsace, and Louis XV furnishings imported from Paris, the opera soon became the veritable symbol of the city. Other construction material came from Italy; besides the Murano glass of the chandeliers, Carrara marble was used for the staircases, statues, and columns. The steel for the walls, on the other hand, was imported from the United Kingdom. Architecture of clearly European inspiration can also be seen in the Art Nouveau Adolpho Lisboa Municipal Market (1882). The so-called Floating Port was Imported from the United Kingdom in 1903. Constructed with both a fixed and a floating section, that is, wharves that could rise or descend as much as 46 feet to adapt to the changing water level during the dry and rainy seasons, it was a technological miracle of its time.

185 The Amazonas Theater in St. Sebastian Square was inaugurated on 31 December 1896. ▷

EVROPA

LUZITANIA

◁ 186-187 *The floating wharves of the Floating Port adapt to the changing level of the waters of the Rio Negro in the dry and rainy seasons.*

△ 187 *Manaus, called the 'green city,' is the capital of ecotourism and the gateway to the Amazon rainforest.*

188 Behind the boy riding his bicycle hang colorful decorations of the residential area of Manaus. △

188-189 Working-class quarters next to tall modern buildings in Manaus are an obvious sign of the strong contradictions characterizing Brazilian society. ▷

EDITORA DO BRASIL
EB
EDITORA DO BRASIL

190 Constructed in 1882, the Adolpho Lisboa Municipal Market is a replica of the former Art Nouveau market, Les Halles, in Paris. △

191 Stained glass frames the entrance to the Adolpho Lisboa Municipal Market. ▷

CARDOSO

BELÉM, THE GATEWAY TO AMAZONIA

The capital of the state of Pará, Belém is one of the gateways to the Amazon rainforest, a starting point for excursions to the island of Marajó and the fascinating boat trip to Manaus. Founded by the Portuguese in 1616, it owes its growth to nearby sugarcane and coffee plantations as well as to the rubber industry.

Today the urban layout of Belém is modern, with tree-lined avenues and highrises that stand besides European Neoclassical buildings (in the Cidade Velha or Old City). A visit to this interesting city can begin with the Forte do Presepio, a fort erected along the right bank of the Amazon River to protect Portuguese property from French and Dutch raiders. The neighboring Catedral da Sé was designed by Giuseppe Antonio Landi, an architect from Bologna, responsible for the many late Baroque and Neoclassical features in the city. Praça da República is the square with the precious Theatro da Paz or Peace Theater (1874), inspired by monumental European theaters and built of precious materials. Inside is a beautifully frescoed hall with an impressive coffered ceiling. In the elegant Nazaré quarter stands the monumental Basilica of Nossa Senhora de Nazaré (Our Lady of Nazareth), designed by the Italian Gino Coppedé in 1909 and modeled after the Basilica of San Paolo in Rome.

◁ 192-193 *Because of its river harbor, Belém, the capital of the state of Pará, is one of the gateways to Amazonia and nearby Manaus.*

194 Belém was founded by the Portuguese in 1616. Thanks to sugar cane, coffee and rubber crops, it became a major crossroads of river trade.

194-195 Neo-Classical buildings blend in perfectly with the city's late Baroque urban structure.

DOS
TABAQUEIRA

PRECIOUS OURO PRETO

Declared a UNESCO World Heritage Site in 1980, Ouro Preto (Black Gold) is the largest and best preserved city in the state of Minas Gerais. Founded in 1711 it was christened Vila Rica or Rich Village because it served as the hub of Brazil's gold rush, sparked by the *bandeirantes* (Portuguese and Brazilian adventurer-explorers) in 1693. Thanks to the wealth that it generated, the city summoned the foremost Brazilian Baroque artists and architects to transform Ouro Preto into an architectural gem. It remains splendidly preserved.

Situated on the slopes of the Serra do Espinhaço Mountains at an altitude of 3609 feet, Ouro Preto is known for its steep, winding, paved streets. Lined with white houses with multicolored doors and windows, its roads lead to small plazas with Baroque churches and elegant buildings. The heart of the city is the Praça Tiradentes—a square named after the pseudonym of a famous Brazilian patriot— which boasts the marvelous Governor's Palace and old city hall as well as a series of fascinating and charming colonial period homes. The nearby Igreja de São Francisco de Assis (Church of St. Francis of Assisi), built in 1766, is one of the most important structures in Brazil. Its elegant façade, decorated with two round bell towers, a steatite medallion, and the double-armed Franciscan cross, is the work of the architect and sculptor Antônio Francisco Lisboa, known as Aleijadinho. The opulent Igreja de Nossa Senhora do Pilar (Church of Our Lady of Pilar) is equally interesting. Its interior is decorated with 957 pounds of gold and silver; of particul note are the portals adorned with volutes, the sculptures of wild birds supporting candelabra, and the hair on the carved figure of Jesus, donated by a worshipper as a token of penitence.

Another characteristic feature of Ouro Preto are numerous stone fountains, built to alleviate the water shortage in the city. Not only do they adorn the city's streets and plazas, but also they bear witness to the magic of time, which here slows downs and comes to a halt.

197 Ouro Preto, in the state of Minas Gerais, has been placed on the UNESCO World Heritage List for its splendid Baroque architecture. ▷

ROTATIVO
E

◁ *198-199 The charming houses in the old town are low and brightly colored with decorated doors and windows.*

▽ *199 The two bell towers of the Church of São Francisco de Assis stand out among the colonial houses.*

◁ 200-201 *A common feature of the citizens of Ouro Preto is their innate creativity, as can be seen in the decoration of their homes.*

▽ 201 *Statues of the women of Bahia looking out windows are a feature that enhances the Baroque—and somewhat naïf—style of contemporary Ouro Preto.*

PARATY, A GEM ALONG THE ATLANTIC

The coastline in this area abounds in peninsulas that jut out into the sea to form captivating isolated beaches surrounded by the tall luxuriant mountains of the Mata Atlântica. This is the splendid setting of the town of Paraty, one of Brazil's best preserved historic gems.

When the first Portuguese colonizers arrived, they were astounded by the beauty of this location, once inhabited by the Guaianá Indians. The town they built became even more precious after the discovery of several rich veins of gold in the adjacent state of Minas Gerais. In the late 17th century, Paraty served as a crossroads between the nearby mines and the capital, Rio de Janeiro, as well as a major port for the gold-laden ships headed to Portugal.

The architecture of Paraty was designed to facilitate commerce and the transport of gold. The city's low altitude (16 feet above sea level) made it possible to allow the tide to flood the streets so that ships could penetrate the innermost areas of town. This advantageous setting granted Paraty great prosperity, allowing the upper classes to build many Baroque churches and sumptuous buildings. Its refined atmosphere and fascinating quality have made it a dazzling example of colonial architecture. The city's irregular cobblestone streets, lined with white buildings with multicolored friezes and grilled windows, blend in perfectly with the surrounding natural scenery. Among the most historically and artistically rich Baroque churches is the Igreja Matriz de Nossa Senhora dos Remédios, (Mother Church of Our Lady of Remedies), rebuilt in 1787 over the ruins of an earlier one. Nossa Senhora do Rosário (Our Lady of the Rosary, 1725) is the church where the slaves were permitted to perform their syncretist rituals, while Nossa Senhora das Dores (Our Lady of Sorrows, 1800) was used by white slave owners.

Modern Paraty is one of the most celebrated and vivacious localities on the coast. Today it is marked by a cosmopolitan atmosphere thanks to artists and writers as well as Brazilian and international chefs, all of whom have settled here to open workshops, clubs, restaurants, and art galleries. Due to this development, the government decided to make Paraty a national historic landmark in 1966—a well-earned recognition for one of the most original pearls in the 'Brazilian necklace.'

203 Paraty, in the state of Rio del Janeiro, lies on a stretch of coastline with peninsulas, beaches, and mountains covered by the Mata Atlântica, or Atlantic Forest. ▷

204 Each of the many churches in Paraty was meant to be used as a place of worship for a different social class or ethnic group. ▽

204-205 The city is the most resplendent and best preserved example of colonial architecture, with fascinating colored buildings lining narrow cobblestone streets. ▷

△ 206 top The rise of tourism has led to the creation of many restaurants, art galleries, and shops featuring local handicrafts.

△ 206 bottom The typical crafts of the city are devoted to traditional religious holiday and Carnival costumes.

▷ 207 A wooden miniature model of an old ship decorates the window of a house.

SURPRISING FORTALEZA

This modern, densely populated 'night owl' city of 3.3 million souls is one of the largest in the country. Situated north of the Sertão Desert and a short distance south of the Equator, Fortaleza is the capital of the state of Ceará, in northeastern Brazil.

Fortaleza was founded in 1637 by the Dutch, who, upon settling there, constructed a fortress (Fort Schoonenborch) around which grew a small village that eventually turned into a genuine town. The fort, which now serves as a military barrack, was later rechristened Fortaleza da Nossa Senhora de Assunção (the Fort of Our Lady of the Assumption) by the Portuguese; hence the city's current name.

A popular tourist attraction, Fortaleza attracts masses of visitors on account of both its vast beaches and charming old town. Perched on a small rise 219 yards from the seaside, the oldest area consists of streets with many curious shops and restaurants, as well as numerous museums, theaters and 'art workshops,' all of which bear witness to the city's eclectic character.

208-209 The seaside and long beaches of Fortaleza, framed by skyscrapers and illuminated by glittering lights. ▷

Among the most visible traces of Fortaleza's glorious past are the 20th-century Metropolitan Cathedral, modeled after the Gothic cathedral in Cologne, Germany, and dedicated to St. Joseph, the patron saint of Ceará, and the 18th-century Igreja do Rosario (Church of the Rosary), which still bears some of its original features, such as the wooden altar and chandeliers.

The historic center is also the home of the Mercado Central or central market, a four-story complex with loads of handcrafted products, and the old public prison, whose cells have been converted into artisan workshops.

The city's lively harbor is famous for the Farol do Mucuripe, a 19th-century lighthouse out of operation since 1957 but now a national historic heritage site and the home of the Lighthouse Museum.

Last but not least, large shopping malls and skyscrapers line the Beira Mar promenade and Fortaleza's principal beaches, such as Praia do Meireles, Praia de Iracema, and the fascinating 3-mile-long Praia do Futuro.

210-211 The old town of Fortaleza, located on a small rise 218 yards from the seaside, is known for its bright colors.

Pirata

◁ *212 Art Nouveau stained-glass windows of the José de Alencar Theater, inaugurated in the early 1900s.*

△ *213 top The theater of Fortaleza is dedicated to José Martiniano de Alencar, one of the most influential 19th-century Brazilian authors.*

△ *213 bottom The Dragão do Mar Cultural Center of Fortaleza.*

BLACK SALVADOR DE BAHIA

When one thinks of Salvador, the capital of the state of Bahia, what comes to mind are 31 miles of luxuriant tropical beaches with palm trees, rocks and stretches of white sand washed by a warm sea. One may also visualize perpetual summer, popular music and the beat of percussion instruments, a lively and cheerful mestizo population, bodies exploding in sensual ritual dances, the aroma of spice and exotic fruit, and, of course, the Bahia Carnival, which lasts an entire week and is the largest and most chaotic street festival in the world.

São Salvador da Bahia de Todos os Santos—the original name of the city founded by the Portuguese in 1549—was modeled after medieval cities such as Lisbon and Oporto in the fatherland, with a commercial port and a residential area elevated on a steep hill. The Portuguese Crown built Bahia as the first city in the 'New World,' and made it the first capital (until 1763) and the first colonial port of Brazil. Menaced by Dutch attacks in the early 1600s, it enjoyed a golden age from the 17th to 18th century. Today, with its 4 million inhabitants, Salvador is the third most populated city in the country after São Paulo and Rio de Janeiro, and the largest in northeastern Brazil.

A gentle city of paved ascents and descents, colonial style houses and buildings with plaster surfaces in sharply contrasting, bright colors, Salvador has 365 churches and basilicas, one for each day of the year—manifesting the power of the Catholic Church in the colonial period and the religious devotion of the people.

Its marvelous urban center is essentially comprised of the Cidade Alta and Baixa (upper and lower city). The former, the historic center known as Pelourinho, holds the largest concentration of colonial architecture in all of Latin America and was placed on the UNESCO World Heritage List in 1984. Perched atop one of the steep hills along the coastline of Bahia de Todos os Santos (All Saints Bay), Pelourinho can be reached from the lower city by elevator—the famous Elevador Lacerda built in 1869-73 according to the design of the engineer Antonio de Lacerda, after whom it was named. The elevator rises 93 yards above the yacht harbor, offering a panoramic view. It conveys passengers to the historic quarter, dazzling in its bright colors and Baroque art, from the Catedral Basílica da Sé—originally a Jesuit monastery holding a wealth of artworks, altars and gold ritual objects—to the even more renowned Church of São Francisco,

215 A Bahia woman at a public telephone wearing a typical Salvador costume. ▷

one of the most richly decorated Baroque churches in the world, which, curiously enough, was dedicated to a saint who preached humility and poverty. The interior is clad throughout with masterfully sculpted and gilt woodwork and is illuminated by a huge, 176-pound silver chandelier. The wooden panels of the ceiling are covered with paintings. Another popular site in the historic center is Largo do Pelourinho, also known as Praça José de Alençar, which received its name from the pillory (*pelourinho*) that stood here during the colonial period. The former theater for displaying the punishment meted out to African slaves before crowds of curious onlookers now emanates peace and beauty, enchanting tourists with its beautiful colonial homes. Near the square is the Igreja de Nossa Senhora do Rosário dos Pretos (Church of Our Lady of the Rosary of Black People), constructed in the 17th century by African slaves and to this day a religious reference point for the local black community. The influence of Africa in Salvador de Bahia can be seen in the faces of its inhabitants, 80% of which are of African descent, as well as in the Candomblé, the age-old religious cult based on African and Christian practices that best represents Brazilian religious syncretism. The black soul of the city also emerges in the *capoeira*, an acrobatic martial art that features feet, legs, rhythm and music, and *axé*, a form of music influenced by Afro-Brazilian and samba rhythms. Traditional Bahia cuisine too includes dishes that typically result from the fusion of Brazilian and black cuisine: *moqueca*, for example, is a dish combining shrimp, coconut and tomatoes and served with rice cooked in coconut milk, while *acarajé* are tapioca flour cakes with shrimp and piquant sauce.

The Cidade Baixa or lower city presents the more modern and commercial facets of Salvador. Exploring the Mercado Modelo, the city's most famous and popular handicrafts market, is quite an experience. This picturesque locale not only serves as a setting for bargaining and consumption, but also pulsates to the rhythm of amazing musical and *capoeira* performances and spectacles. The leading attractions in this part of the city are the Igreja de Nossa Senhora da Conceição (Church of Our Lady of the Immaculate Conception), the Admiralty building, and the São Marcelo Fort, which seems to float in the middle of the old harbor. A small round structure built in 1650 on a sand bank, it once had 54 cannons positioned in a fan-like arrangement and is now the home of a historical museum dedicated to the fort and the city.

217 The fort of Santo Antônio da Barra, known as the Farol da Barra, stands out on a headland separating the inner bay from the Atlantic Ocean. ▷

ReVita
solvi

◁ *218-219 Salvador is a labyrinth of narrow, hilly streets and brightly colored buildings that go well with the traditional clothes of the local population.*

POUSADA
VILLA
Casa
Vila Bela

220-221 The highly colorful historic center, known as Pelourinho, is situated in the upper part of the city.

BAHIA
DA BAHIA
LEMBRANÇA
DO SENHOR

◁ *222 'Bonfim' ribbons are votive offerings and requests for protection and good luck offered to the Christ of the Church of Nosso Senhor do Bonfim (Our Lord of the Good End).*

△ *223 Baroque, Rococo and colonial styles merge with the various cults celebrated at the Church of Nosso Senhor de Bonfim.*

224-225 The streets of Pelourinho are full of life at all hours of the day.

CENTRO DE CULTURAS
POPULARES E IDENTITÁRIAS
SECRETARIA DE CULTURA DO ESTADO DA BAHIA
DINHO ARTES

NOSSA SEN
DOS PRETO
MEGA LIQUIDAÇÃO

Color, Rhythm and Traditions

Brazil's cultural identity moves hand in hand with its history. Although forged by Portuguese domination, the country absorbed a broad gamut of elements from aboriginal populations, Africans, and the many immigrants from Europe, the Middle East, and Asia. Indigenous tribes contributed to the creation of modern Brazil through their idiomatic languages, legends, music, and dance. When the Portuguese arrived in the 16th century, they encountered 700 indigenous dialects (today 180 are still spoken by fewer than 600 persons), which, over the course of time, influenced the language of the early colonists. Although Portuguese became the official language in 1759, other languages helped enrich its vocabulary. Various idiomatic expressions, as well as the present names of animals and plants, derive from *tupi-guarani*, spoken by certain local peoples. Other terms were borrowed from African dialects, such as the word *samba*, which derives from the Angolan word *semba*, one of the meanings of which is 'belly-touching.'

Immigration had an impact not only on the development of the language, but also on Brazilian customs and religions. We need only mention the cult of Candomblé and *capoeira*, both of which originated among black slaves wishing to retain their identity, and which later became foundation stones of Brazil's profoundly multicultural culture.

The wealth of history, languages, and traditions in Brazil has also influenced the imagination of Brazilian writers who have contributed to the creation of a major literary tradition. Thanks to their many publications and numerous editions of novels, poetry, and plays, one can safely say that half the literary production of Latin America comes from Brazil. Significant historical events have often served as the content and inspiration for literary works. Initially, in the colonial period (from the early 16th century to Brazilian independence in 1822), they generated a Baroque and Arcadian style. Later, independence from the mother country coincided with the rise of the Romantic movement and the exaltation of concepts such as liberty, subjectivity, and the cult of the motherland. The Symbolist movement of the second half of the 19th century witnessed the rise of allegorical and metaphorical poetry, which was

226 A brightly colored float in the Rio Carnival.

227 A woman wearing typical white Candomblé ritual clothing.

229 Brazil is a melting pot of ethnic groups, nationalities, traditions, and religions, all of which have contributed to the country's rich culture.

CUIDADO...
PROGRESSO

REPLACED IN THE 20TH CENTURY BY A STRONGER AVANT-GARDE SENSIBILITY AND MODERNISM. IN THE WAKE OF THESE MOVEMENTS, SUBJECTS RELATED TO BRAZILIAN FOLKLORE, TRADITION, HISTORY, AND SOCIETY WERE PROUDLY EVOKED, NARRATED, BUT ALSO CRITICIZED, BY AUTHORS SUCH AS JOÃO GUIMARÃES ROSA AND JORGE AMADO. THE 'BARD' OF *SAUDADE*, THE BRAZILIAN VARIANT OF THE MOOD OF NOSTALGIC REGRET OR PROFOUND SOLITUDE, AMADO WROTE NOVELS PERMEATED WITH TYPICALLY LATIN AMERICAN VIGOR AND FERVOR TO BECOME THE COUNTRY'S GREATEST LITERARY PHENOMENON.

ANOTHER OF BRAZIL'S CULTURAL FOUNDATION STONES IS SOCCER, DEEMED TO BE THE ONLY TRULY UNIVERSAL RELIGION IN THE COUNTRY, WHICH, BEGINNING WITH PELÉ, HAS PRODUCED A LONG LIST OF TALENTED PLAYERS. MATCHES HERE APPROACH 'MYSTICAL' EVENTS, IN WHICH FANS PARTICIPATE BODY AND SOUL, WITH JOY AND SORROW, AND THUS SHARE IN A UNIQUE AND GREAT FORM OF COLLECTIVE ECSTASY.

◁ *230-231 In Brazil, football is considered a religion 'practiced' by the entire population.*

CANDOMBLÉ AND FESTIVALS: RELIGIOUS SYNCRETISM

Although Brazil has the largest Catholic community in the world and Catholicism is its official religion, the country is also known for its syncretic cults and variety of sects, which offer much freedom to their observers.

The roots of Brazilian religion lie in the animism practiced by native populations, in Catholicism, and in African cults, that is, Candomblé, which was introduced by blacks slaves. This last of these religions arose when the European colonists prohibited the slaves from practicing their religions and also banned music and dancing for fear that such arts would reinforce their identity and pride. Such intolerance simply served to spark the development of widespread syncretism. In order to avoid persecution, slaves gave Catholic names and identities to the Orixás, the African spirits and divinities associated with elements of nature. In this way they were able to continue worshiping their own divinities under the guise of Catholic saints.

In the 19th century, religious freedom became one of the tenets of Brazil's constitution. Nonetheless, African beliefs continued to be subject to severe discrimination for a long time. To the white ruling class, Candomblé was synonymous with charlatanism and ignorance and associated with the poorest social strata. Nowadays such prejudices are a thing of the past. Indeed, in Bahia and Rio de Janeiro huge groups of Afro-Brazilian cult followers gather on New Year's Eve and New Year's Day to celebrate as millions of Brazilians go to the beach to pay homage to Yemanja, the goddess of the sea, by offering her flowers, perfume, fruit, and even jewels in order to obtain her protection and blessings.

In the meantime, the religious spectrum of Brazil has gradually broadened to include Indian animism, African-Catholic syncretism, and the spiritualism of Allan Kardec, a French pedagogue who founded a cult based on belief in reincarnation. Various more or less extremist deviations exist as well: Umbanda or white magic, which mixes a type of spiritualism typical of the Bantu rituals of Angola with Candomblé, and Quimbanda or macumba, a form of black magic, whose violent rituals are illegal.

233 Yemanja, the goddess of the sea, is one of the major divinities of the Candomblé religion, the most popular Afro-Brazilian cult in the country. ▷

◁ 234-235 *The followers of the Candomblé religion venerate Orixas, African divinities associated with the elements of nature, who must be honored with offerings, sacred dances, and songs.*

△ 235 *Colorful flowers are a must in Brazilian religious processions, which have become part and parcel of this country's folk traditions.*

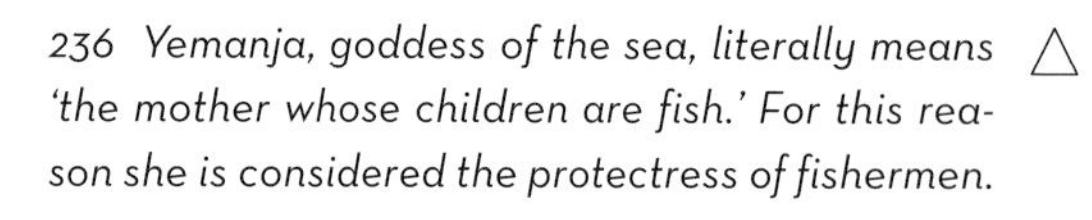

236 Yemanja, goddess of the sea, literally means 'the mother whose children are fish.' For this reason she is considered the protectress of fishermen. △

236-237 The celebration of Yemanja's feast takes place on February 21 in Salvador de Bahia with the participation of followers of the Candomblé religion as well as Catholics and non-religious persons. ▷

238 In addition to Candomblé, animist cults of Indian origin, the spiritism of Allan Kardec, various forms of white magic, and sometimes even black magic are practiced in Brazil. △

238-239 In animist rituals, participants dress in white before being possessed by Orixa divinities. ▷

CAPOREIRA: MARTIAL ART AND DANCE OF THE SLAVES

The *capoeira* is a martial art disguised as an acrobatic dance in which four competitors engage in a combat of self-defense. It originated about four centuries ago, when Afro-Brazilian slaves took to performing ritual dances in order to defend themselves against colonists and plantation owners but also to train themselves for potential escape from the plantations. For this reason the *capoeira* was prohibited and outlawed in the *senzalas*, or slave barracks. Consequently, the slaves began practicing the sport secretly or, by adding rhythm and music, pretending it was merely an acrobatic dance. Even after the abolition of slavery, this often violent sport remained clandestine; indeed, *capoeiristas* were registered as suspects in police records. The 1930s marked the turning point; searching for an activity that might serve as the national sport, the government of President Getúlio Vargas gave Manoel dos Reis Machado (known as Mestre Bimba) permission to open the first *capoeira* academy, which led to the discipline's institutionalization as a form of artistic expression.

Today there are two types of *capoeira* in Brazil: the slow and relatively peaceful *capoeira Angola*, named after its country of origin and made popular by Mestre Pastinha; and the more aggressive *capoeira regional*, launched by Mestre Bimba and developed on the plantations of Cachoeira and other cities in the region of Recôncavo, close to Salvador.

Contemporary *capoeira* is a combination of a martial art, a game, and a dance. Its movements are always fluid and circular, and the competitors, who exchange make-believe blows, are respectful and playful. The exhibition takes place between two 'fighters' inside a circle or *roda* comprised of other fighters and spectators who clap their hands and sing during the 'battle.' The clapping and the sound of the *berimbau* (a single-stringed musical instrument resembling a fishing pole) were once a way of warning the competing slaves that the landowner was arriving. At a later stage they were integrated into the dance to maintain the rhythm. Besides the *berimbau* the game is accompanied by the *pandeiro* (hand frame drum), *agogô* (bell), and *atabaque* (tall drum).

Every year the *capoeira* attracts more and more aficionados, who train along the huge beaches or in improvised street *rodas*—a perpetual spectacle that emits and transmits great energy.

241 Created four centuries ago by African slaves as a form of self-defense, the capoeira has evolved into a combination of martial art, play and dance. ▷

242-243 Beaches are the most interesting and suitable settings for the capoeira, which nowadays is performed in two versions: slow and relaxed, or aggressive and fast-paced. ▷

CARNIVAL, MULTICOLORED FOLLY

Sensuous dancers, fabulous costumes, overwhelming music, and a blaze of colors—these are the basic ingredients of the Brazilian Carnival, the largest street celebration in the world. Albeit Brazilian, the Carnival originated in Europe. In the Middle Ages, certain European countries held rowdy festivals to celebrate the period right before Lent. According to some scholars, the word 'carnival' derives from the Latin expression *carnem levare*, meaning the abstinence (*levare*) from meat (*carnis*) and other worldly pleasures required throughout Lent. One of the most widespread Carnival festivals was the Entrudo, which originated on the Azores and became popular in Lisbon and the Portuguese colonies. This was a street festival that sometimes turned violent when black slaves assailed each other with eggs, oranges and flour, while white spectators threw buckets of water.

The uninhibited Entrudo arrived in Brazil in the 16th century and became an ever more integral part of Brazilian social life. Banned for over two centuries because of its violence, it was resumed by a group of dock workers in Salvador de Bahia who performed in folk groups called *ranchos* in Rio de Janeiro and organized the first parades set to march music (*marchinha*). Initially, the Carnival did not have a truly representative musical tradition; melodies and rhythms were simply improvised. Only in the 19th century did the event acquire its own elegant musical style, thanks to the introduction of the European masked ball in Brazil. Indeed, by 1834, the art of the masquerade had become widespread due to the importation of French wax or paper masks representing animal heads.

In 1885, the first floats organized by Carnival groups—the *clubes*—were introduced to Rio. Fourteen years later the first piece of music composed expressly for the occasion came into being: Chiquinha Gonzaga's march, *Ó Abre Alas*. The real revolution occured in the 1920s, with the spread of a new musical genre, the samba. The first samba school, 'Deixa Falar' or 'let me speak,' was founded in Rio in 1927. Five years later, another school, Estação Primeira de Mangueira, won the first official prize at the Brazilian Carnival.

245 The three principal components of the Carnival in Brazil are the samba, colorful costumes, and exuberance. ▷

The 1930s were the golden age of the samba, so much so that the dance spread from the working-class quarters at the center of Rio and began to diversify into a spectrum of different styles that evolved over time into *bossa nova*, a combination of samba and jazz that utilizes rhythm in a more melodious fashion, and finally Tropicalism, with its less elegant but more heterogeneous sounds.

The Rio Carnival has also formalized its complicated choreographic structure, making it obligatory for the various groups that participate in the parade. Meanwhile, other Brazilian cities have imposed their distinguishing features onto their own carnivals. Consequently, the festival has come to be celebrated in different ways and with different rhythms depending on where it is held. Thus we have the samba in Rio de Janeiro, *axé* and *afoxé* in Salvador, and *frevo* and *maracatu* in Recife. Furthermore, while in Rio there are innumerable floats accompanied by percussionists and dancers who celebrate all night long in stadiums built expressly for this purpose, in Salvador, the festivities take place in the streets, where bands play on huge trucks equipped with powerful loudspeakers. In Olinda, in turn, the old town is filled with gigantic papier mâché puppets, people in costume, and musical ensembles. Porto Alegre, Florianópolis, Corumbá, Ouro Preto, and many other Brazilian cities and towns organize festivals with live music shows, gallons and gallons of *cachaça* liquor, and guaranteed fun and entertainment. Whatever the case, Carnival is an event deeply rooted in the heart and soul of the Brazilian people, who prepare for it with intensity and delight. Indeed, millions of volunteers work tirelessly all year long, making costumes and organizing and staging dances so that their groups may win the hosted competitions. The samba schools in Rio, the Afro-Brazilian *trios eléctricos* in Salvador, the *blocos de frevo* at Recife, which are supported by tens and even hundreds of thousands of members, have become the social and cultural point of reference for the citizens of these metropolises, sometimes even replacing inadequate government organizations.

◁ *246 Hundreds of volunteers work full-time for an entire year planning and making the costumes, decorations, and other elements of the parade.*

248 The Carnival arrived in Brazil as a festival imported from Lisbon to the Portuguese colonies in the 16th century. △

249 The first Carnival floats in Rio de Janeiro made their appearance in 1885, while rigorous rules for the choreography of the parade were established in 1950. ▷

250-251 From the 1920s on, the samba spread as a new musical genre in Brazil; its lively rhythms and dances marked a turning point in the Carnival.

Você, sem fronteiras.
NÃO

◁ 252-253 *A basic ingredient of every Carnival is sensuality. Many of the festivities conclude with a prize for the most beautiful girl in the parade.*

COFFEE, THE BLACK RESOURCE OF THE LAND

As strong as the Devil, as hot as hell, and as sweet as love. This is how Brazilians want their coffee, one of the mainstays of the country's diet, and a source of energy that one cannot do without. Whereas in the morning, Brazilians drink it with milk (*cafè com leite*), during the day they prefer a *cafezinho*, black coffee served in a glass or demitasse, often already sweetened. Coffee originated in Abyssinia and was introduced by the Dutch in their colonies; it arrived in Brazil only in 1727, via Dutch Guyana (Suriname), and was soon cultivated on a large scale. Although it made its first appearance in the state of Pará, it became more popular in the state of Rio, and by the early 19th century already amounted to 18% of the country's total exports. Two episodes in particular underlay the 'coffee boom:' the political crisis in the French colony of Haiti (a leading coffee producer) and the 'economic independence' espoused by Emperor Pedro II (1844), who aimed at reducing importation. Thanks to coffee exportation, Brazil had a favorable balance of payments in foreign trade for the first time between 1860 to 1885. Paraíba Valley became the richest region in the country, but the shortsighted policy of deforestation aimed at creating more land for cultivation provoked a climatic change that actually made the region unsuitable for this crop. Consequently, most cultivation of the bean shifted to the state of São Paulo, where sugar cane plantations were supplanted by ones growing coffee, considered more profitable. The construction of a railway line along the coastal mountain range made it possible to transport large quantities of coffee to the port of Santos, from which ships took it to markets throughout the world. The industry also led to the creation of a powerful Brazilian caste of 'coffee men,' who have exerted a profound influence on the country's political history. The crisis of manual labor from Africa triggered by the abolition of slave traffic in 1888 was overcome by the encouragement of European immigration, including hordes of people from Italy. The next wave, which ended ca. 1930, included many Japanese. At the beginning of the 20th century, coffee accounted for over 60% of exports. Thanks to the industry's success, Brazil became a leading participant in intercontinental commerce. Today the country holds the world record in coffee production, and much of its national economy is rooted in the plantations, often comprised of a few enormous estates.

255 After coffee beans are picked, they are dehydrated, either through a dry or wet process.

256 Brazil's hot, humid climate is ideal for the cultivation of coffee plants. △

256-257 Artificial irrigation on a coffee plantation. ▷

RIDE YOUR BRAIN WAVES
profesional

◁ *258-259 The coffee beans are spread outdoors and left to dry before being selected for the roasting process.*

△ *259 Roasted coffee is delicate and must be kept in special sacks, protected from oxygen and light, and, if possible, at a low temperature.*

PINHALENSE

◁ *260-261 Roasting is the final phase in the preparation of coffee beans; the process imparts flavor to the raw bean, which is relatively tasteless.*

▽ *261 Nowadays Brazilian coffee is produced in about 80 different varieties and is one of the country's principal resources.*

THE INDIOS: A FRAGILE PAST

22 April 1500—the day on which the Portuguese explorer and colonizer Pedro Álvares Cabral and his men set foot in Brazil—marked the beginning of the gradual extinction of the country's indigenous populations, which had subsisted on agriculture and hunting. At the time, they numbered between two and four million and were divided among three principal groups: the Guaraní, the Tupi, and the Tapuia. Many of the natives fell victim to the *bandeirantes*, wandering adventurers who pillaged and destroyed any village they came across while exploring the interior. Those who managed to escape European violence ended up either decimated by diseases brought by the colonists, or reduced to slavery on sugarcane or coffee plantations. What sheer physical decimation did not do was 'compensated' by the cultural destruction wrought by early Jesuit missionaries, who banned the practice of local customs, traditions, and religions, and forced the Indios to live in *aldeias* (missions) after dispossessing them of their territory.

More recently, since the early 1980s, warnings of the danger of the potential extinction of the remaining 300,000 natives in Brazil have led the local government and international community to enact projects and programs to protect the rights, land, and traditions of those Indios who still live in the country in about different 60 tribes.

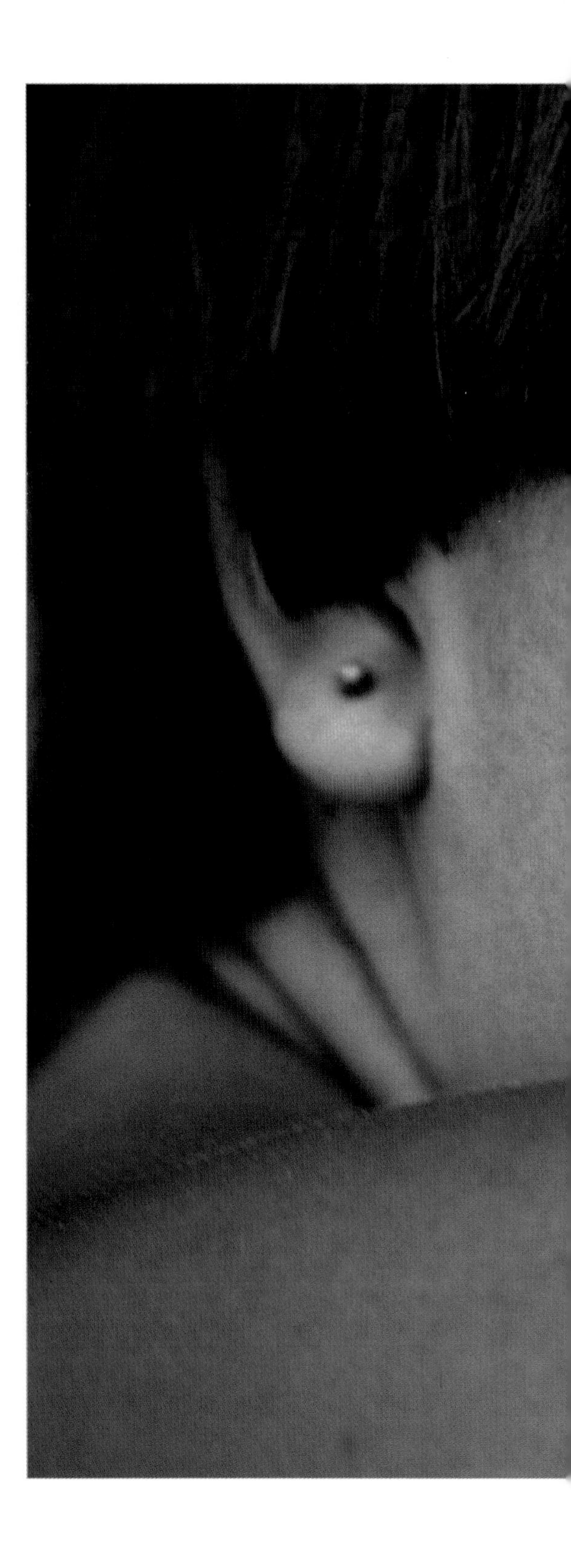

262-263 The Yanomami are an ethnic group. Most of them live in the forest between the basins of the Orinco and Amazon Rivers. ▷

264 *Today there are about 300,000 Indios in Brazil distributed among approximately 60 tribes that still live in harmony with their pristine environment.* ▽

264-265 *The Matis are skillful hunters who manage quite well in the thick Amazon forest.* ▷

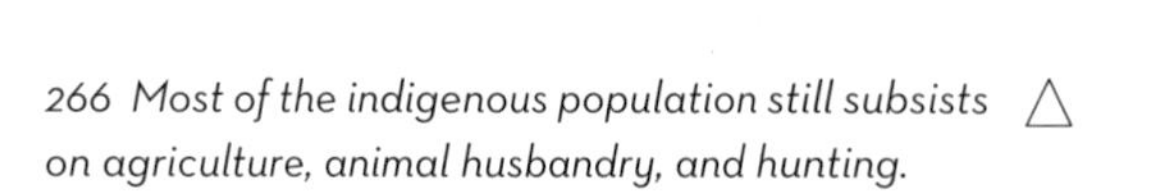

266 Most of the indigenous population still subsists on agriculture, animal husbandry, and hunting.

266-267 A young Indio in his wooden dugout canoe.

Index

c = caption
bold type = chapter

Photographic credits

Peter Adams/AWL Images/Getty Images: pages 224-225
Peter Adams/Getty Images: pages 155, 218-219
AFP/Getty Images: pages 174, 248
Theo Allofs/Ramble/Age Fotostock: pages 86-87
Theo Allofs/Zefa/Corbis: pages 74-75
Cecilia Alvarenga/Getty Images: page 199
Joedson Alves/dpa/Corbis: pages 23, 120-121
Keiny Andrade/LatinContent/Getty Images: pages 230-231
Marco Andras/Age Fotostock/Marka: pages 213 bottom, 210-211
Giulio Andreini: pages 197, 233
Antonello/Getty Images: page 201
Apic/Hulton Archive/Getty Images: page 26
Yann Arthus-Bertrand/Corbis: page 50
Atlantide Phototravel/Corbis: page 215
Lou Avers/dpa/Corbis: pages 112-113
Ricardo Azoury/Olhar Imagem: page 156
John Banagan/Age Fotostock: pages 129, 142-143, 198-199, 145
David Bank/JAI/Corbis: pages 176-177
Barnabas Bosshart/Corbis: page 227
Judy Bellah/Getty Images: page 144
Catarina Belova/Shutterstock: pages 108, 156-157
Jefferson Bernardes/Stringer/Getty Images: page 124 bottom
Bettmann/Corbis: pages 36-37, 39
Biosphoto/SuperStock: page 49
Massimo Borchi/Atlantide Phototravel/Corbis: pages 120, 168-169
Rodrigo Baleia/LatinContent/Getty Images: pages 52-53
Luiz Felipe Castro/Flickr Open/Getty Images: pages 164-165
Yasuyoshi Chiba/AFP/Getty Images: page 190
Heeb Christian/Prisma/Age Fotostock: pages 84-85, 149, 152, 154, 194-195
G. Dagli Orti/De Agostini Picture Library: pages 25, 28-29, 30
James Davis/Eye Ubiquitous/Corbis: page 116
Ricardo De Mattos/Getty Images: page 217
Michael DeFreitas/Robert Harding World Imagery/Corbis: page 185
Cicero Dias Viegas/Tips Images: page 213 top
Celso Diniz/123RF: pages 136-137
Celso Diniz/Shutterstock: page 161
De Agostini Picture Library: pages 22, 24, 27, 29, 30-31, 32, 32-33, 35
Silvio Dutra/Olhar Imagem: pages 20-21
David Evans/National Geographic Society/Corbis: pages 255, 256
Andrea Florence/ardea.com: pages 68-69
Owen Franken/Corbis: pages 266-267
Nick Garbutt/naturepl.com/Bluegreen: pages 78-79
Bertrand Gardel/hemis.fr/Getty Images: page 203
Globo/Getty Images: page 38
Nick Gordon/naturepl.com/Bluegreen: pages 264-265
Steve Heap/Shutterstock: pagg. 80-81
Robert Holmes/Corbis: page 261
Jeremy Horner/Corbis: page 109
Richard I 'Anson/Lonely Planet Images/Getty Images: pages 6-7, 44, 226, 250-251
ImageSource/Age Fotostock: page 89
Ammit Jack/Shutterstock: page 62
Jaynes Gallery/DanitaDelimont.com: page 64
Jon Arnold Images/Danita Delimont.com: page 93
Held Jürgen/Prisma/Age Fotostock: page 127
Ita Kirsch/Brazil: pages 68, 76 top, 76 bottom, 79 bottom, 186-187 bottom
Zig Koch/Olhar Imagem: pages 47, 54-55
Florian Kopp/imagebroker/Age Fotostock: pages 124 top, 148, 152-153
Frans Lanting/National Geographic: pages 12-13, 45
Thiago Leite/Shutterstock: pages 162-163, 166
Yadid Levy/Age Fotostock: pages 206 top, 206 bottom
Yadid Levy/Robert Harding World Imagery/Corbis: page 249
Diego Lezama Orezzoli: pages 125, 259
Diego Lezama Orezzoli/Corbis: pages 256-257, 260-261
Mauricio Lima/AFP/Getty Images: page 41
LookImages/Cuboimages: page 212
Benjamin Lowy/Getty Images: pages 258-259
Alessandro Lucena/Flickr Open/Getty Images: page 222
Frank Lukasseck/Zefa/Corbis: page 74
luoman/Getty Images: pages 4-5
luoman/iStockphoto: page 266
Roberto Machado/Tips Images: pages 98-99
Alfredo Maiquez/Lonely Planet Images/Getty Images: pages 220-221
Malven/iStockphoto: page 55
Filipe Matos Frazao/Shutterstock: page 67
Buda Mendes/LatinContent/Getty Images: page 131
Mary Ann McDonald/NHPA/Photoshot: page 77
Loren McIntyre/Stock Connection/Age Fotostock: page 58
Morales/Age Fotostock: pages 58-59, 61
Dorival Moreira Lucin/Keystone RM/Age Fotostock: pages 188-189, 192-193
Sebastiao Moreira/epa/Corbis: pages 42-43
nataliejorge/iStockphoto: pages 182-183
News Free/CON/LatinContent/Getty Images: pages 16-17
Richard T. Nowitz/Corbis: pages 130-131
Paulo Oliveira/123RF: pages 94-95
Oktay Ortakcioglu/iStockphoto: pages 241, 242-243
ostill/123RF: page 207
ostill/iStockphoto: page 118
Pete Oxford/naturepl.com/Bluegreen: pages 64-65, 73
Lucio Ruiz Pastor/Age Fotostock: pages 200-201
Frilet Patrick/hemis.fr/Getty Images: page 100-101
Frilet Patrick/Hemis/Corbis: page 99
Michel Pellanders/Hollandse Hoogte/Contrasto: pages 262-263, 264
Andrea Pistolesi: pages 188, 204, 204-205
Andrea Pistolesi/Tips Images: page 194
Celso Pupo/Shutterstock: page 11
Harald von Radebrecht/imagebroker/Age Fotostock: pages 88-89
Radius Images/Marka: pages 2-3
Morley Read/123RF: page 60
Rogerio Reis/Olhar Imagem: page 183
Romulo Rejon/Flickr Open/Getty Images: page 223
Geoff Renner/Robert Harding World Imagery/Corbis: page 119
Alf Ribeiro/SambaPhoto/Getty Images: pages 172-173
Robin Utrecht Fotografie/HillCreek Pictures/Corbis: pages 252-253
Alex Robinson/JAI/Corbis: page 103
Luiz Rocha/Shutterstock: pages 132-133, 134-135

Ricardo Rollo/Abril Comunicações s.a. : page 83
Eliano Rossi/Corbis: page 236
Evaristo Sa/AFP/Getty Images: page 187
SambaPhoto/Cristiano Mascaro/ Getty Images: page 129
SambaPhoto/Eduardo Barcellos/ Getty Images: page 167
Robert A Sanchez/iStockphoto: page 63
Kevin Schafer/Minden Pictures/ Corbis: pages 70-71
Mark Schwettmann/Shutterstock: page 132
Lamberto Scipione/Keystone RM/ Age Fotostock: pages 117, 191
Antonio Scorza/AFP/Getty Images: pages 245, 246
Pietro Scozzari/Age Fotostock: pages 146-147
Marco Simoni/Robert Harding Picture Library/Age Fotostock: page 147
Slow Images/Photographer's Choice/ Getty Images: pages 18-19
Jan Sochor/LatinContent Editorial/Getty Images: pages 234-235, 236-237
Alina Solovyova-Vincent/Getty Images: page 229
G. Sosio/De Agostini Editore/Age Fotostock: page 87
Raul Spinasse/dpa/Corbis: pages 235, 238
Michal Staniewski/Shutterstock: page 140
George Steinmetz/Corbis: pages 8-9, 91
Super Stock/Age Fotostock: page 143
Jane Sweeney/Lonely Planet Images/Getty Images: pages 170, 171
M&G Therin-Weise/Age Fotostock: pages 56-57
tunart/Getty Images: pages 208-209
Masa Ushioda/RHPL/OKAPIA: pages 104-105
João Vianna/Flickr/Getty Images: pages 102-103, 106-107
View Pictures/Universal Images Group/Getty Images: pages 178-179, 179
Peeter Viisimaa/Getty Images: page 150-51
John Warburton-Lee/ DanitaDelimont.com: pages 50-51, 122-123, 140-141
JohnWarburton-Lee/Cuboimages: pages 96-97, 180-181
Alan Weintraub/Arcaid/Corbis: pages 138-139, 173
Staffan Widstrand/naturepl.com/ Bluegreen: pages 72-73
Alexandre Wittboldt/ SambaPhoto/Getty Images: page 175
Priscila Zambotto/Flickr/Getty Images: page 168

Cover
The renowned architect Oscar Niemeyer conceived the futuristic Contemporary Art Museum in Rio de Janeiro as a flower blossoming from a vase, represented by the pool of water below.
© Alan Weintraub/Arcaid/Corbis

Back cover
Iguaçu Falls, in the state of Paraná, are among the most amazing water spectacles in all of Brazil.
© Richard I 'Anson/Lonely Planet Images/Getty Images

Author

Simona Stoppa a professional journalist, specializes in naturalistic, tourist, marine and anthropological themes. She is an author and writer of television formats of a documentary and journalistic nature and produces corporate films for a variety of companies. She writes for Touring Club Italiano and for Edizioni White Star, in addition to collaborating with various magazines and websites. She teaches television communication at the Università Cattolica in Brescia and is involved in corporate counseling with the use of audio-visual tools for the purpose of training paths in empowerment, team-building and teamwork.

PROJECT EDITOR
Valeria Manferto De Fabianis

EDITORIAL ASSISTANT
Giorgia Raineri

GRAPHIC DESIGN
Maria Cucchi

WS White Star Publishers® is a registered trademark property of De Agostini Libri S.p.A.

© 2014 De Agostini Libri S.p.A.
Via G. da Verrazano, 15
28100 Novara, Italy
www.whitestar.it - www.deagostini.it

Translation: Richard Pierce
Editing: Irina Oryshkevich

All rights reserved. No part of this publication may be reproduced, stored in a retrieval system or transmitted in any form or by any means, electronic, mechanical, photocopying, recording or otherwise, without written permission from the publisher.

ISBN 978-88-544-0821-0
1 2 3 4 5 6   18 17 16 15 14

Printed in Italy